STA

Please return / renew by date shown.
You can renew it at:
norlink.norfolk.gov.uk
or by telephone: 0344 800 8006
Please have your library card & PIN ready

NORFOLK COUNTY LIBRARY
WITHDRAWN FOR SALE

NORFOLK LIBRARY
AND INFORMATION SERVICE

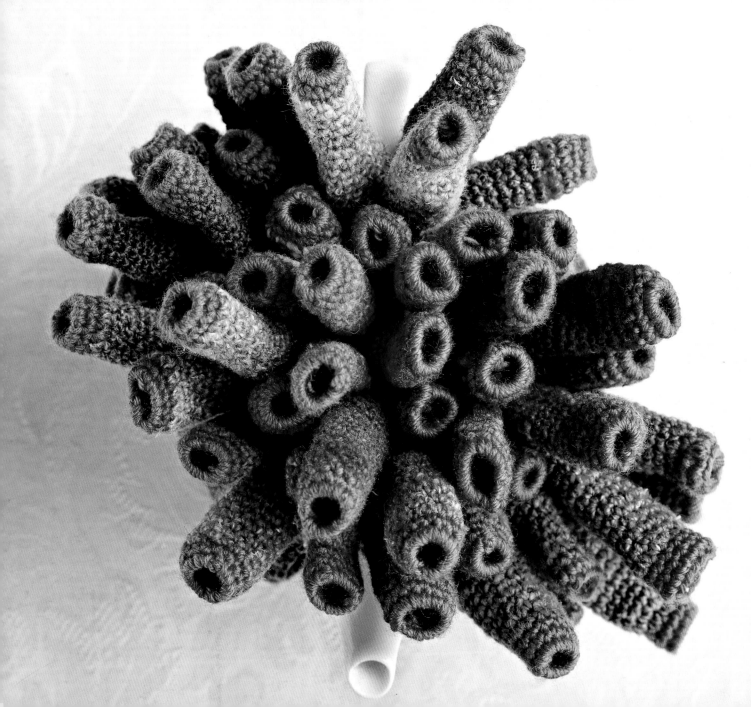

For my mother, Kate, who would have smiled so wide.
And for my son Benjamin, who makes ME smile so wide.

really
wild tea cosies
Loani Prior

MURDOCH BOOKS

Contents

Introduction

Tea cosies are funny 7

Tips and techniques

Knitting in the round on
two sets of circular needles 8

To line or not to line 13

Measuring up – the right teapot 14

Your stash 14

Colour 14

Felt good 15

Blocking 15

Only some of the answers 15

Tea cosies

The Jester 16

Coral Punk 21

Garden Party 24

Pablo 31

Bells & Mexicans 36

Elfin 43

Nanna Deluxe 46

Still Life 51

Modern Primitive 54

Grecian Lovely 61

Loopy Lou 64

Roger Rampant 71

Pedro de la Pantaloon 76

Sleeveless In Seattle	85
Up in Arms	88
Mongolian Sock Warriors	93
Little Miss Cupcake	96
Pot Sock Frock and Petticoat	103
Hanky Panky	106
Ode to the Lime	111
Short Black with Two	114

Flowers and other fun stuff

Rose (knitted)	118
Short Leaf	120
Long Leaf	121
Rose (crocheted)	123
Trumpet Flower	124
Gumnuts	125
Cupcake	126
Felted balls	128
I-cord	129
Citrus Fruit	130
Cushion	131
Pompoms	132
Scarf	133
Abbreviations	134
Conversion tables	134
Acknowledgments	135

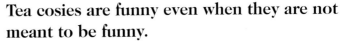

Tea cosies are funny

Tea cosies are funny even when they are not meant to be funny.
And tea POTS are very accommodating. They will not bemoan your handmade gift. They will not worry about the colour suiting their complexion, or that it doesn't quite fit. There will be no prissiness about scratchy wool. They will not say 'how lovely' and then hide it at the back of a cupboard somewhere.
Make a teapot smile. Knit a cosy.

Nothing complicated
Some of the tea cosies in this little book might LOOK complicated to the beginning knitter. But they are NOT complicated at all. The cosies that look complicated are made up of a number of very simple components, each leading you to a beautifully constructed knitted sculpture.
If there is some technique you are not familiar with, how perfect to try it out on a tea cosy. Don't be shy! Have a go! You'll feel very pleased with yourself.

Tips and techniques

Knitting in the round on two circular needles

Once you have mastered this technique, you will never want to knit in the round in any other way. Or conversely, you will lose your mind and never knit again. There are two very good reasons for trying out this method. Firstly, there are only two joins instead of four, as with double-pointed needles, and secondly, the join is seamless, without the laddered stocking ridge that occurs at the point of needle change as with double-pointed needles.

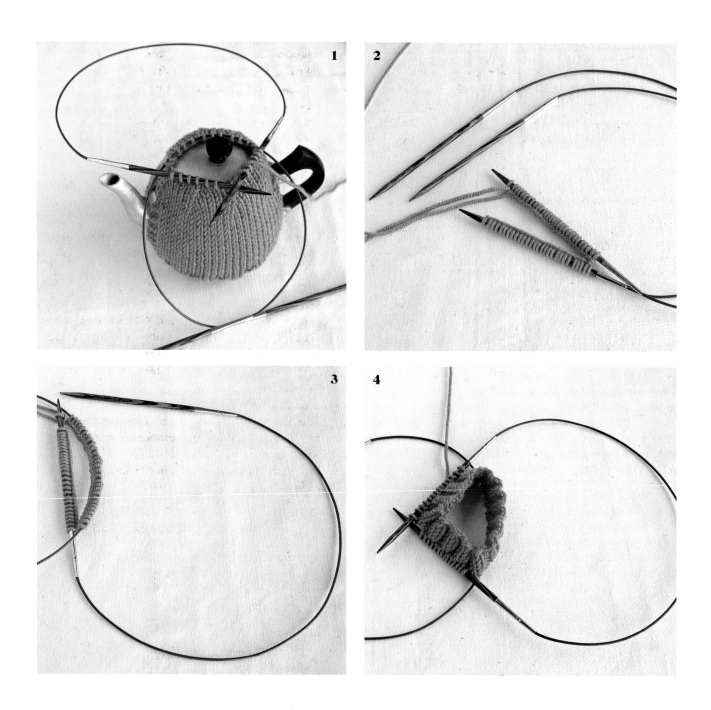

1. Like life, really

The most important thing to remember when using this method is that there is always a WORKING circular set and a SLEEPING circular set of needles. You are constantly alternating between the two circular sets.

It is only the yarn that goes round and round. By keeping the non-working stitches dangling out of the way on the flexible section of the sleeping circular set, you always know which stitches you're meant to be knitting. It's just a matter of alternating sleeping and working – like life, really.

2. Casting On

Cast on the desired number of stitches (plus one extra stitch) onto one set of circular needles. Now transfer the first half of the stitches onto the second circular set, leaving the extra stitch on the circular set holding the working thread. Push all the stitches down the needles to the other end to get access to the working thread again. Ensure that the stitches are not twisted around the needles.

3. Joining in the Round

** To join the stitches into a round, move the extra stitch (at the point where the working thread is) to the other circular set. The circular set that now holds the extra stitch is now your working set. Pick up your working circular set and knit the first two stitches together (the extra stitch and first cast on stitch) creating a firm join.

You have just completed the only fiddly bit to the operation.

Note. You only need to make the extra stitch when you are joining at cast-on or when joining two tea cosy sides together again. You will NOT make an extra stitch each time you move from one circular set to the other circular set. You are already 'joined'.

4. Working in ROUNDS

When you finish knitting to the end of the stitches held on this circular set, immediately pull the needle through so that the stitches just worked are now sitting on the flexible section with the needle points dangling – the new sleeping circular set.

Pick up the previously sleeping circular set and pull the stitches back onto the needle point to meet with the working thread. With the new working circular set, knit all its stitches.

Continue knitting in the round in this fashion until you have the desired number of rounds.

5. Working in ROWS

To begin working the first side, work back across the stitches you have just made, using the same working circular set. You will now work in rows, not rounds. When Side One is complete, move the stitches to the flexible part of the circular set, to sleep while you attend to the other side of the tea cosy.

6. Joining in the thread to Side Two

If you began Side One with the wrong side facing (e.g. a purl row in stocking stitch), then you need to begin the second side with the wrong side facing also. Work Side Two in ROWS.

7. Joining in the round again at the handle

To begin working in ROUNDS again, you will need to make the extra 'joining' stitch at the point where the working yarn is. The simplest way is to frog back one stitch, then knit into the front and back of the last stitch on that side.

Follow the instructions from **.

8. Joining in the round again at the spout

You will need to add an extra 'joining' stitch at this end too and repeat as for Step 7. Continue to work in the round, alternating circular sets.

A tip: When changing from one set of needles to the other, make the first stitch and then pull the yarn firmly downwards to tighten the join between the two needles. This simple action will eliminate ridges at the needle changeover point.

TO LINE OR NOT TO LINE

To line or not to line, that is the question. The answer is … LINE! Always make a lining if the pattern states. *Really Wild Tea Cosies* is filled with little knitted sculptures. Some are a bit weighty on top. A lining under the cosy body will give strength and extra warmth. And mostly importantly, it will look its very best.

Measuring up — the right teapot

Yes, yes. I know in my introduction I said that teapots are very accommodating, but...teapots come in all shapes and sizes and I strongly advise you to have your pot in front of you the whole time, so that you can measure your work against it.

Not all three-cup teapots are the same shape. Some are squat and plump. Some are tall and thin. Some have their spouts halfway down the belly. Some have their spouts at the very top of the belly. If your tea cosy doesn't look the same as the one in the picture, it most likely has to do with the shape of your teapot – oh, yes – and the difference in your tension. You could make a tension (gauge) swatch but then, you almost have one side of a tea cosy. If it is not measuring up, pull it undone and add or subtract stitches. If you know yourself to be a loose knitter, use a smaller needle size than suggested in the patterns.

Most cosies should fit snugly and curvaceously over the pot. They should not ride up like a bad mini skirt. Neither should they fall about like an old man's jumper.

Your stash

You can never have too much wool. Go on. Say it. 'I can never have too much wool.' There now. Doesn't that feel better? It is your paint palette, your woodpile, your clay blocks. You can't possibly let your imagination run wild without lots of beautiful yarns to enrapture you.

Colour

If you ever needed an excuse to go wild with colour, the little tea cosy provides it. In fact, the tea cosy demands it. Think bright, luminescent and fluorescent. Think primary, think rainbow. Think cabaret, carnival, festival. Your tea cosies want to be centre stage. They want to hog the limelight. They DESERVE it.

Felt good

You need to buy wool that says 'gentle hand wash in cold water' and then do the opposite. The Nundle Woollen Mill 8-ply Collection and the Noro Kureyon collection felt up beautifully. They have the happiest of happy colour palettes that would do any tea cosy proud and they felt like a dream.

I stand at the kitchen sink dressed in my favourite pink rubber gloves, the ones with faux leopard skin cuffs. I fill the sink with water as hot as my gorgeously gloved hands can stand and with a cake of soap agitate the tea cosy to within an inch of its life.

Dry the cosy to its proper shape over the teapot or a cardboard cut-out shape (See the cone shape of Elfin, on page 43). When the tea cosy is completely dry, repeat the process if needed.

Blocking

I don't always block, but sometimes it can be the making of a tea cosy. The Mongolian Sock Warriors were at a distinct disadvantage without blocking.

Lightly dampen the knitted tea cosy. Dampen an old towel, lay it folded in half on a table and pin the tea cosy to the towel. It should be pinned in as many spots as possible. When all is in perfect symmetrical order, lay a flap of the wet towel on top and leave it to dry for the next couple of days.

One could just iron it, but it isn't advisable. The heat of the iron has an unhappy effect on wool, flattening the fibres into unpleasantness. Blocking is definitely the go.

Only some of the answers

My little book is not meant to be a teacher of knitting techniques, so if anything is not explained as well as you'd like, please take the time to look up other books or search the web. YouTube has some great teaching videos about every conceivable knitting and crochet technique.

Some of my patterns, the ones I thought might be tricky for the beginner, have alternative easy versions, so read through to the end before you begin knitting

Remember, the funny old tea cosy is perfect for trying out new techniques. Don't be shy! Have a go!

I love this tea cosy.
It is just so … funny!

The Jester
{Knitted cosy}

SIZE
To fit a four-cup teapot that stands 12 cm (4¾ in) tall (not including the knob) and 13 cm (5 in) in diameter (not including the spout and handle).

MATERIALS
- Two 50 g (1¾ oz) balls Noro Kureyon wool, colour of your choice (Main Colour, MC)
- Two 50 g (1¾ oz) balls Nundle Collection 8-ply wool, Contrast Colour (CC): Yellow

EQUIPMENT
- Two sets 5 mm (UK 6, US 8) circular needles, 60 cm (24 in) long from needle tip to needle tip
- Large stitch holder or third circular needle
- Darning needle
- Scissors
- Your favourite rubber gloves
- Soap

JESTER PEAKS (MAKE 2)
Worked in ROUNDS from the top down.
Using one strand of Noro Kureyon wool (MC) and both sets of 5 mm (UK 6, US 8) circular needles, cast on 7 stitches (6 sts plus 1 st for joining in the round), placing 3 stitches on one circular needle and 4 stitches on the other circular needle. Refer to **Knitting in the round on two sets of circular needles**, on page 8, to join.

Rounds 1–4: Knit.
Begin first increasing pattern (12 rounds):
Mark the beginning of the round with a short length of contrasting coloured yarn. This is essential, otherwise confusion will reign supreme. It did for me.
Round 5: Increase once in first stitch, K5.
Round 6 (and each alternate round): Knit to end of round.
Round 7: K4, increase once in next stitch, K2.
Round 9: Increase once in 1st stitch, K7.
Round 11: K5, increase once in next stitch, K3.
Round 13: Increase once in 1st stitch, K9.
Round 15: K6, increase once in next stitch, K4 (12 sts).
Round 16: Knit to end of round.

Note. Now is the time to add in the yellow yarn. It is carried across the back of the work, woven into the back of every second stitch until it is needed again for the stripe. It is this 'weaving' that gives the lovely yellow dash pattern at the rolled up edge around the bottom of the cosy. It also makes the knitted fabric a lot sturdier than if knitted without.

Here is a great opportunity to try a new technique. Or you could ignore the stripe altogether at the knitting stage and sew a yellow stripe on when the knitting is finished.

Round 17: *K1 (CC), K1 (MC), repeat from * to end of round.
Begin second increasing pattern, including yellow stripe.
Round 18 (increasing): *K1 (CC), increase once in next stitch using MC, repeat from * to end of round.
Rounds 19–25: *K1 (CC), K2 (MC), repeat from * to end of round.
Round 26 (increasing): *K1 (CC), K1 (MC), increase once in next stitch using MC, repeat from * to end of round.
Rounds 27–33: *K1 (CC), K3 (MC), repeat from * to end of round.

Round 34 (increasing): *K1 (CC), K2 (MC), increase once in next stitch using MC, repeat from * to end of round.
Rounds 35–41: *K1 (CC), K4 (MC), repeat from * to end of round.
Round 42 (increasing): *K1 (CC), K3 (MC), increase once in next stitch using MC, repeat from * to end of round.
Rounds 43–49: *K1 (CC), K5 (MC), repeat from * to end of round.
Round 50 (increasing): *K1 (CC), K4 (MC), increase once in next stitch using MC, repeat from * to end of round.
Rounds 51–57: *K1 (CC), K6 (MC), repeat from * to end of round.
Round 58 (increasing): *K1 (CC), K5 (MC), increase once in next stitch using MC, repeat from * to end of round (48 sts).
Rounds 59–65: *K1 (CC), K7 (MC), repeat from * to end of round.

Transfer these 48 stitches to a large stitch holder or to a third circular needle for keeping until later, while you make the second Jester Peak.

JESTER BODY
Now that you have two Jester Peaks, transfer all the stitches from one Jester Peak onto one 5 mm (UK 6, US 8) circular needle and all the stitches from the other Jester Peak to the other 5 mm (UK 6, US 8) circular needle.
Knitting a seam
To knit the two Jester Peaks together, hold the two sets of circular needles parallel to each other with the tips pointing in the same direction and the right (knit) sides facing each other.
Insert the working needle knitwise into the first stitch on the front needle and the first stitch on the back needle. Loop the yarn around the working needle and draw it back through the two stitches and off the circular needles held in the left hand.

Repeat this instruction one more time. Now you have two stitches on the working needle. To cast off, bring the first stitch up and over the second stitch and off the working needle. Now you have one stitch on the working needle. Repeat until you have cast off 25 stitches.

Pop that last stitch onto one of the circular needles so that you have 23 stitches on each.

Knitting a seam too complicated?
If you are not comfortable with knitting the seam together, simply cast off 25 stitches on each of the Jester Peaks and sew the seam together when all the knitting is finished.

Shaping the sides
You are now knitting in ROWS.

Side One
Row 1 (right side facing): Using MC, ssk, K4, increase once in next stitch, K1 (CC); using MC, increase once in next stitch, **K5, increase once in next stitch, K1 (CC); using MC, increase once in next stitch, knit to last 2 stitches, K2tog.

Hint for the following increasing pattern:
You are decreasing at the beginning and end of the row. And you are increasing before and after the two yellow stripes.
Row 2 (and each alternate row): Purl, continuing to weave and work the stripe in CC yarn as you go.
Row 3: As for **Row 1**, except at **, K7.
Row 5: As for **Row 1**, except at **, K9.
Row 7: As for **Row 1**, except at **, K11.
Row 9: As for **Row 1**, except at **, K13.
Row 11: As for **Row 1**, except at **, K15.
Row 13: As for **Row 1**, except at **, K17.
Row 14: Purl, continuing to weave and work the stripe in CC yarn as you go.
Leave stitches on needle. Break off yarn.

Side Two
Join in yarn to stitches on other needle and work Side Two to correspond with Side One.

Lower Body
Join the two sides into a round again (see **Knitting in the round on two sets of circular needles**, on page 8) and knit 6 rounds.
Cast off.

FINISHING
Darn in ends. Make two small yellow pompoms (see page 132) and stitch one to the tip of each Jester Peak.

Designing this cosy was like being in chocolate heaven. What colour next? Devouring the little balls of lusciousness. Then wrapping them all up in a sea of blue. Throw caution to the wind! Breathe in. Breathe out. And start crocheting. You can do it because the 'doing' is so satisfying and the result is spectacular. This is organic, feral, freeform (call it what you like) crocheting and there is only one rule to follow: have the teapot in front of you at all times. No two Coral Punks will be the same.

Coral Punk

{Crocheted cosy}

SIZE
I made my cosy to fit a two-cup teapot that stands 9 cm (3½ in) tall (not including the knob) and 12 cm (5 in) in diameter (not including the spout and handle).

MATERIALS
- Two 50 g (1¾ oz) balls Noro Kureyon Sock wool: Ah! So many colours to choose from …
- One 50 g (1¾ oz) ball 4-ply wool: Pink

EQUIPMENT
- 3 mm (UK 11, US D/3) crochet hook
- Darning needle
- Scissors

Note. American crocheters, please check the **Crochet Abbreviations and Conversions** *table on page 134.*

CORAL TENDRILS

Using a 3 mm (UK 11, US D/3) hook and 4-ply pink wool, make 7 chain. Sl st into first chain to close the circle. Make 2 ch (counts as first dc). Make 12 dc into the circle, join with a sl st to first st. Continue working in the round until desired length, working the first 3 rounds in pink before changing colour. There are three general sizes: small, medium and large, the largest being as long as my index finger.

When you have five or six tendrils of the same hue and of different sizes, sew them together at the base. The first three or four might be a bit fiddly but it gets easier and easier as it grows. Don't be too precious about it. It will all work out beautifully in the end.

My first intention was to cover the entire two-cup teapot with tendrils, but feeling well-sated at 51, it was time to drink tea and think sea.

BLUE OCEAN BODY

Remember! You have thrown caution to the wind. Toss the tendril mass over the top of the teapot in a rakish manner. Mark the tendril sitting at the spout with a contrasting coloured thread.

Begin the blue ocean base by outlining the tendril mass with a round of dc stitch, gathering the tendril edges into as much of a straight line as possible.

Look long and hard at the photograph. There are straight edges and angled lines. Crochet the rows of dc stitches as if you are colouring in shapes. Always start with the straight edge hugging the spout or the handle.

Straight edges

To make a straight edge, make 2 ch (counts as first dc). Miss the last dc of the last row and dc into the next stitch. When you come back to this straight edge, make your last dc stitch into the space made by the 2 ch in the previous row.

Angled lines

To make an angled line, dc to the last 2 stitches before the end of the row. Sl st into the next stitch. Turn. Miss the sl st of the previous row. Sl st into the next dc, then dc to end.

Keep measuring and shaping against the teapot. Measure and shape, measure and shape!

If it is clearly not working out, pull it back and start again. Unlike knitting, there is only one stitch to pick up. But again, don't be too precious about it.

Base

Once you have covered the bowl of the teapot on both sides, join in a round by crocheting straight across from one side to the other. To achieve the flat doily effect at the base of the tea cosy, make 2dc into every fifth or sixth stitch. If it is not sitting flat to the table, increase more often. If it is curling up into a frilly wave, increase less often.

FINISHING

Darn in any ends.

If you've made Coral Punk for a friend, be sure to photograph it in natural daylight before you let it go. Mine has been my computer desktop picture for the past six months. It makes my heart smile all day long.

Pretty. Pretty. Pretty. Garden Party may LOOK complicated, but she's NOT. She is clever in her simple detail. It is all the little things that count. She is covered in lots of lovely simple little flowers and things made with love and arranged with style.

Garden Party

{Knitted body, lining and tray;
knitted and crocheted flowers}

SIZE

To fit a four-cup teapot that stands 13 cm (5 in) tall (not including the knob) and 12 cm (4½ in) in diameter (not including the spout and handle).

MATERIALS

- One 50 g (1¾ oz) ball Jo Sharp DK Tweed: Asparagus (Body)
- One 50 g (1¾ oz) ball Nundle Collection 8-ply wool: Olive (Lining and Tray)
- Scraps of different coloured yarn for Flowers, Leaves and Gumnuts – I have used Noro Kureyon and Noro Kureyon Sock wool, but this could be the perfect opportunity to use up your stash leftovers
- Polyester fibrefill (optional)

Note. Noro Kureyon comes in many beautiful shades. You are best to choose your favourite colours from your nearest yummy craft store, or on-line.

EQUIPMENT

- Two sets 5 mm (UK 6, US 8) circular needles, 60 cm (24 in) long from needle tip to needle tip (Body/Lining)
- One pair 4 mm (UK 8, US 6) regular knitting needles (Roses and Leaves)
- 3 mm (UK 11, US D/3) crochet hook (Trumpet Flowers)
- 4 mm (UK 8, US G/6) crochet hook (Gumnuts)
- Scissors
- Darning needle

BODY AND LINING

The cosy and lining are worked in one piece, which is then folded in on itself to create the lining.

The basket-weave pattern is a multiple of 8 stitches and 10 rows.

Remember! You will be working in ROUNDS and then in ROWS and things change.

Lower Body

Using both sets of 5 mm (UK 6, US 8) circular needles and two strands of Jo Sharp DK Tweed yarn, cast on 65 stitches (64 sts plus 1 st, for joining in the round), placing 32 stitches on one circular needle and 33 stitches on the other circular needle. Refer to **Knitting in the round on two sets of circular needles**, on page 8, to join.

Rounds 1–5: *K4, P4, repeat from * to end of round.
Rounds 6 and 7: *P4, K4, repeat from * to end of round.
Mark the 'right' side of the work with a piece of yarn in contrasting colour.

Divide for sides as follows:
Side One

Now you will begin to work in ROWS not rounds. To start working in rows, turn the work so that you are working back across the stitches you have just made, keeping the basket-weave pattern correct.

Row 1: *P4, K4, repeat from * to end of row.
Row 2: *P4, K4, repeat from * to end of row.
Row 3: *P4, K4, repeat from* to end of row, thus completing the 10-row basket-weave pattern.
Rows 4–8: *K4, P4, repeat from * to end of row.
Rows 9–13: *P4, K4, repeat from * to end of row.
Rows 14–18: *K4, P4, repeat from * to end of row.
Rows 19 and 20 (2 rows only): *P4, K4, repeat from * to end of row.
Leave stitches on needle. Break off yarn.

Side Two

Join the two strands of yarn to the stitches on the other needle and work Side Two to correspond with Side One.

Upper Body

Referring to **Knitting in the round on two sets of circular needles**, on page 8, join the two sides together into a round again and continue in basket-weave pattern for 8 rounds.
(DO NOT cast off.)

LINING

Change to Nundle 8-ply yarn, using only a single thread.

Upper Body

Rounds 1–8: *K1, P1, repeat from * to end of round (1x1 rib).

Divide for the sides as follows:
Side One

Now you will begin to work in ROWS not rounds. To start working in rows, turn the work so that you are working back across the stitches you have just made. Work Side One in 1x1 rib, as before, in ROWS for 18 rows.
Leave remaining stitches on needle. Break off yarn.

Side Two

Join in yarn to the stitches on the other needle and work Side Two to correspond to Side One.

Lower body

Referring to **Knitting in the round on two sets of circular needles**, on page 8, join the two sides together into a round again. Continue in 1x1 rib for 6 rounds. Cast off loosely.

FLOWERS

You will find all flower patterns beginning on page 118.

Amazingly, the length of yarn required to make one flower is almost exactly the length of yarn from colour change to colour change in the Noro Kureyon range. Choose the flower colour palette for vibrancy and variation.

Knitted Roses: Make 5
Trumpet Flowers: Make 5
Short Leaves: Make 5
Long Leaves: Make 1
Gumnuts: Make 3

GARDEN TRAY

If your teapot lid is flat, you can give your flower garden some lovely height by making two trays. Lay the trays, one on top of the other like pancakes, sew the edges together and stuff with a little polyester fibrefill.

Using both sets of 5 mm (UK 6, US 8) circular needles and Olive 8-ply yarn, cast on 15 stitches (14 sts plus 1 st, for joining in the round), placing 7 stitches on one circular needle and 8 stitches on the other circular needle. Refer to **Knitting in the round on two sets of circular needles**, on page 8, to join.

Round 1: Knit to end of round.
Round 2: *K1, increase once in next stitch, repeat from * to end of round.
Round 3 (and each alternate round): Knit to end of round.
Round 4: *K2, increase once in next stitch, repeat from * to end of round.
Round 6: *K3, increase once in next stitch, repeat from * to end of round.
Round 8: *K4, increase once in next stitch, repeat from * to end of round.
Round 10: *K5, increase once in next stitch, repeat from * to end of round.

Round 12: *K6, increase once in next stitch, repeat from * to end of round.

Round 14: *K7, increase once in next stitch, repeat from * to end of round.

Round 16: *K8, increase once in next stitch, repeat from * to end of round.

Round 17: Knit to end of round.

Before you cast off, try it on your teapot, with the sock body, for size. If it is not quite big enough, continue in the increasing pattern until it is the desired size.
Cast off.

PUTTING IT ALL TOGETHER

Darn in all ends. Fold the lining section of the body to the inside, aligning the openings for the spout and handle. Oversew the lining and the outer body together around the edges of the spout and handle openings.

Place the tea cosy body over the teapot with the folded edge at the top. Pin the Garden Tray into place (8 rounds below the top rim) and sew into position, securing it to both the inner and outer sock walls, thus creating a flat rim around the tray. I like to use a simple tacking stitch from inside to outside.

Now you need to draw on all your excellent flower arrangement skills. Before sewing anything into place, arrange, arrange, arrange (see top-down view on page 27). Use pins. If you think you need more flowers, make more flowers. The flowers need to cover the entire tray, bursting out of their knitted vase.

When you are happy, peel away everything but the Leaves. Sew them into place. Arrange, arrange, arrange the flowers again. Peel away everything but the Roses and sew them into place. Arrange, arrange, arrange again; peel away everything but the Gumnuts and sew them into place. Finally, arrange the Trumpet Flowers and sew them into place.

Oh, many an art historian has pondered the origins of Cubism. But it is a little known fact that it was Picasso's grandmother, Nanna Picasso, who changed the course of European art, well before Pablo was a twinkle in his father's eye.

This original Nanna Picasso tea cosy, circa 1860, not only kept the young Pablo's tea warm on a summer's afternoon, but also proved to be a radical influence on his art and the avant-garde art movement of the early 20th century.

Pablo

{Knitted cosy and lining}

SIZE

To fit a four-cup teapot that stands 13.5 cm (5¼ in) tall (not including the knob) and 14.5 cm (5¾ in) in diameter (not including the spout and handle).

MATERIALS

- 3 x 50 g (1¾ oz) balls Nundle Collection 8-ply wool, Main Colour (MC): Mustard
- 1 x 50 g (1¾ oz) ball Nundle Collection 8-ply wool, Contrast Colour (CC): Orange
- Polyester fibrefill

Note. Nundle wool felts beautifully. If varying your yarn, choose 100% pure wool that felts well.

EQUIPMENT

- Two sets 4 mm (UK 8, US 6) circular needles, 60 cm (24 in) long from needle tip to needle tip (see *Note*, below)
- 3 clothes pegs
- Darning needle
- Scissors
- At least 9 large wooden beads
- Rubber bands
- Your favourite rubber gloves
- Soap

Note. Circular needles can be used for knitting the flat sides as well, although you can use regular knitting needles if you prefer.

OUTER BOX SIDES – VARIATION 1 (MAKE 2)

I have made two sides with orange SQUARES (Variation 1) and two sides with orange STRIPES (Variation 2). You might prefer to have all the sides the same as each other. The sides with squares use a combination of Intarsia (or bobbin) and Fair Isle (or weaving) techniques. The sides with stripes are worked from side to side rather than bottom to top and you simply change colour when you get to that row. If you really think you will have trouble with the weaving technique, use the striped variation for all the box sides.

Cut 3 lengths of Orange wool (CC), each measuring 2.1 metres (83 in). Wrap one length of yarn around each of the 3 pegs, to use as bobbins. Leave peg balls of yarn aside for the moment.

Using Mustard wool (MC) and one set of 4 mm (UK 8, US 6) circular needles, cast on 40 stitches.
Row 1: *K1, P1, repeat from * to end of row.
Row 2: *P1, K1, repeat from * to end of row.
These 2 rows form moss stitch pattern.
Row 3: K1, P1, knit to last 2 sts, P1, K1.
Row 4: P1, K1, purl to last 2 sts, K1, P1.
Row 5: K1, P1, knit to last 2 sts, P1, K1.
Row 6: P1, K1, purl to last 2 sts, K1, P1.
Row 7 (begin Orange squares): K1, P1, K2; join in first peg ball of Orange (CC) yarn and K8 (CC), at the same time weaving MC along the back of your work; drop first ball of CC; K4 (MC); join in second peg ball of CC and K8 (CC), weaving MC as before; drop second ball of CC; K4 (MC); join in third peg ball of CC and K8 (CC), weaving MC as before; drop third ball of CC; using MC, K2, P1, K1.
Row 8: Using MC, P1, K1, P2, pick up CC and P8 (CC), weaving in MC along 'front' of work ('front' is the work facing you as you purl); drop CC; P4 (MC); pick up second ball of CC and P8 (CC), weaving MC as before; drop CC; P4 (MC); pick up third ball of CC and P8 (CC),

weaving MC as before; drop CC; using MC, P2, K1, P1.
Repeat rows 7 and 8 three more times to complete the first line of Orange squares.
Row 15: Using MC, K1, P1, knit to last 2 sts, P1, K1.
Row 16: P1, K1, purl to last 2 sts, K1, P1.
Row 17: K1, P1, knit to last 2 sts, P1, K1.
Row 18: P1, K1, purl to last 2 sts, K1, P1.
Repeat rows 7 to 18 two more times.
Row 43: *K1, P1, repeat from * to end of row.
Row 44: *P1, K1, repeat from * to end of row.
Cast off.

OUTER BOX SIDES – VARIATION 2 (MAKE 2)

As you look at the photo, the striped sides that look as though they were knitted from bottom to top, are actually knitted from side to side and are extremely easy.

Using 8-ply Mustard wool (MC) and one set of 4 mm (UK 8, US 6) circular needles, cast on 40 stitches.
Row 1: *K1, P1, repeat from * to end of row.
Row 2: *P1, K1, repeat from * to end of row.
These 2 rows form moss stitch pattern.
Row 3: K1, P1, knit to last 2 sts, P1, K1.
Row 4: P1, K1, purl to last 2 sts, K1, P1.
Row 5: K1, P1, knit to last 2 sts, P1, K1.
Row 6: P1, K1, purl to last 2 sts, K1, P1.
Rows 7–14: Change to Orange wool (CC) and repeat Rows 3–6 two more times.
Rows 15–18: Change to MC and repeat Rows 3–6 once.
Repeat rows 7–18 two more times.
Row 43: *K1, P1, repeat from * to end of row.
Row 44: *P1, K1, repeat from * to end of row.
Cast Off.

OUTER BOX TOP (MAKE 1)

Cut 2 lengths of Orange wool (CC), each measuring 2.1 metres (83 in). Wrap one length of yarn around each of 2 pegs, to use as bobbins. Leave peg balls of yarn aside.

really wild tea cosies

Using Mustard wool (MC) and one set of 4 mm (UK 8, US 6) circular needles, cast on 30 stitches.

Row 1: *K1, P1, repeat from * to end of row.
Row 2: *P1, K1, repeat from * to end of row.
These 2 rows form moss stitch pattern.
Row 3: K1, P1, knit to last 2 sts, P1, K1.
Row 4: P1, K1, purl to last 2 sts, K1, P1.
Row 5: K1, P1, knit to last 2 sts, P1, K1.
Row 6: P1, K1, purl to last 2 sts, K1, P1.
Row 7 (begin Orange squares): K1, P1, K3. Join in first peg ball of Orange (CC) yarn and K8 (CC), at the same time weaving MC along the back of your work; drop first ball of CC; K4 (MC); join in second peg ball of CC and K8 (CC), weaving MC as before; drop second ball of CC; using MC, K3, P1, K1.
Row 8: P1, K1, P3; pick up CC and P8 (CC), weaving in MC along 'front' of work ('front' is the work facing you as you purl); drop CC; P4 (MC); pick up second ball of CC and P8 (CC), weaving MC as before; drop CC; using MC, P3, K1, P1.
Repeat rows 7 and 8 three more times to complete the first line of Orange squares.
Row 15: K1, P1, knit to last 3 sts, P1, K1.
Row 16: P1 K1, purl to last 3 sts, K1, P1.
Row 17: K1, P1, knit to last 3 sts, P1, K1.
Row 18: P1, K1, purl to last 3 sts, K1, P1.
Repeat rows 7 to 18 two more times.
Row 43: *K1, P1, repeat from * to end of row.
Row 44: *P1, K1, repeat from * to end of row.
Cast off.

LINING

Remember! You will be working in ROUNDS and then in ROWS and things change.

Lower Body

Using both sets of 4 mm (UK 8, US 6) circular needles and Mustard 8-ply wool, cast on 81 stitches (80 sts plus 1 st, for joining in the round), placing 40 stitches on one circular needle and 41 stitches on the other circular needle. Refer to **Knitting in the round on two sets of circular needles**, on page 8, to join.

Rounds 1–10: *K2, P2, repeat from * to end of round (2x2 rib).

Divide for sides as follows:
Side One
Now you will begin to work in ROWS not rounds. To start working in rows, turn the work so that you are working back across the stitches you have just made.
Row 1 (wrong side): K4, purl to last 4 sts, K4.
Row 2 (right side): Knit to end of row.
Repeat these 2 rows 12 more times (26 rows in all, for spout and handle openings).
Leave remaining stitches on needle. Break off yarn, leaving a long thread for darning in later.

Side Two
With the wrong side facing, join in yarn to the stitches on other needle and work Side Two to correspond with Side One.

Crown
Begin working in rounds again, referring to **Knitting in the round on two sets of circular needles**, on page 8.
Rounds 1–4: Knit to end of round.
Round 5: *K8, K2tog, repeat from * to end of round.
Round 6: Knit to end of round.
Round 7: *K7, K2tog, repeat from * to end of round.
Round 8: Knit to end of round.
Round 9: *K6, K2tog, repeat from * to end of round.
Round 10: Knit to end of round.
Continue in this decreasing pattern until 8 stitches remain. Break off yarn and, with a darning needle, thread the end through the remaining stitches. Pull up tightly to close.

PUTTING IT ALL TOGETHER

It is the sewing together of the rectangles that helps give the tea cosy its cubed shape. Place two sides together with the right sides facing out. I used a simple tacking stitch to accentuate the edges. Match up the other two rectangles and sew together.

Sew the two right-angled sides to the top square, again with the right side facing you while you sew them together.

To help measure the spout and handle opening, you should 'do a fitting' on the tea pot. Place the Inner Cosy on the pot. Place some fibrefill inside the lid of the cube, filling up the corners to give it its cubed shape. Place this over the Inner Cosy and pin up the spout and handle seams ready for sewing.

Sew the remaining seams using a short tacking stitch.

Sew the outer cosy to the lining around the spout and handle openings.

FELTING

Darn in all ends and felt all the rectangle pieces before joining. Do not felt the Cosy Lining.

Place a wooden bead in the middle of the wrong side of an orange square, stretching the knitted material over the bead. Secure in place with a rubber band. Repeat for all orange squares on each rectangle. On Variation 2 (stripes), centre 3 beads along the stripe at equal intervals and hold in place with rubber bands. If you don't have masses of wooden beads, you'll just have to be patient and felt each rectangle, one at a time.

Felt the rectangles before constructing the cubed tea cosy. Follow the felting instructions on page 15 and leave the wooden beads in place during the felting process until the knitted fabric is dry.

The success of this tea cosy is all about colour. Choose well and luxuriate in the result. The difference between the two styles of cosy is not in the knitting. The pattern for each is exactly the same. The difference is only in the placing of the plastic cone insert. That's all. Magic.

Bells & Mexicans

{Knitted cosy and lining}

SIZE
To fit a three-cup teapot that stands 10 cm (4 in) tall (not including the knob) and 13 cm (5 in) in diameter (not including the spout and handle).

MATERIALS
- 1 x 50 g (1¾ oz) ball Nundle Collection 8-ply wool, Main Colour (MC): Cerise
- 1 x 50 g (1¾ oz) ball Nundle Collection 8-ply wool, Contrast Colour 1 (CC1): Orange
- 1 x 50 g (1¾ oz) ball Noro Kureyon, Contrast Colour 2 (CC2)
- Hard plastic sheet (see *Note*)

EQUIPMENT
- Two sets 4 mm circular needles (UK 8, US 6), 60 cm (24 in) long from needle tip to needle tip
- Scissors
- Darning needle
- Masking tape or staples

Note. You could use cardboard, but it might get soggy with the heat of the tea in the pot. A sheet of sturdy plastic will do the job better, something found around the house – the back of a ring-bound document holder perhaps.

BODY

The Body and the Bell are knitted in one piece, then folded into shape around the plastic insert.

Remember! You will be working in ROUNDS and then in ROWS and things change.

Lower Body

Using both sets of 4 mm (UK 8, US 6) circular needles and MC, cast on 81 stitches (80 sts plus 1 st, for joining in the round), placing 40 stitches on one circular needle and 41 stitches on the other circular needle. Refer to **Knitting in the round on two sets of circular needles**, on page 8, to join.

Rounds 1 and 2: *K2, P2, repeat from * to end of row (2x2 rib).
Round 3: *K2 (MC), P2 (CC2), repeat from * to end of round. (Carry the threads very loosely across the back of the work, leaving room for elasticity in the finished knitted fabric.)
Continue the striped ribbed pattern (Round 3) for 7 more rounds.

Divide for sides as follows:

Side One

Now you will begin to work in ROWS not rounds. To start working in rows, turn the work so that you are working back across the stitches you have just made. Working in ROWS, continue the striped rib pattern up the first side of tea cosy for 20 rows. Leave stitches on needle. Break off yarn, leaving a long length to darn in later.

Side Two

With the wrong side facing you, join the yarn to the first stitch on the other circular needles. Work Side Two to correspond with Side One.
Break off the CC2 yarn to darn in later.

really wild tea cosies

Upper Body

With the right side facing, begin working in the round again, referring to **Knitting in the round on two sets of circular needles**, on page 8.

Round 1: Using MC only, knit to end of round.

Round 2: K2tog to end of round.

Rounds 3–7: *K1, P1, repeat from * to end of round. (DO NOT cast off.)

BELL

Round 8 (increasing): *Increase once in next stitch (MC), K1 (CC1), repeat from * to end of round. (The second knit stitch gives a clean colour change from one round to the next.)

Rounds 9–12: *K2 (MC), P1 (CC1), repeat from * to end of round.

Round 13 (increasing): *K2 (MC), increase once in next stitch (CC1), repeat from * to end of round.

Rounds 14–17: *K2 (MC), P2 (CC1), repeat from * to end of round.

Round 18 (increasing): *K2 (MC), increase once in next stitch (CC1), P1 (CC1), repeat from * to end of round.

Rounds 19–22: *K2 (MC), P1 (CC1), K1 (MC), P1 (CC1), repeat from * to end of round.

Round 23 (increasing): *K2 (MC), P1 (CC1), increase once in next stitch (MC), P1 (CC1), repeat from * to end of round.

Rounds 24–29: *K2 (MC), P1 (CC1), K2 (MC), P1 (CC1), repeat from * to end of round.

Round 30: Change to Noro Kureyon (CC2) and knit to end of round (for a clean colour change).

Round 31: Purl to end of round (to give a neat folding edge).

You should now have 120 stitches, 60 stitches on each circular needle.

Rounds 32–35: *P2, K1, P2, K1, repeat from * to end of round.

Round 36 (decreasing): *P2tog, K1, P2, K1, repeat from * to end of round (100 sts).

Rounds 37–40: *P1, K1, P2, K1, repeat from * to end of round.

Round 41 (decreasing): *P1, K1, P2tog, K1, repeat from * to end of round (80 sts).

Rounds 42–45: *P1, K1, P1, K1, repeat from * to end of round.

Round 46 (decreasing): *K2tog, P1, K1, repeat from * to end of round (60 sts).

Rounds 48 and 49: *K1, P1, K1, repeat from * to end of round.

Round 50 (decreasing): *K2tog, K1, repeat from * to end of round (40 sts).

Rounds 51 and 52: Knit to end of round.

Round 53 (decreasing): K2tog to end of round (20 sts).

Round 54: Knit to end of round.

Round 55 (decreasing): K2tog to end of round (10 sts).

Round 56: Knit to end of round.

Break off yarn and, with a darning needle, thread end through the remaining stitches, draw up tightly and darn into the wrong side of the work.

LINING
Lower Body

Using both sets of 4 mm (UK 8, US 6) circular needles and MC, cast on 73 stitches (72 sts plus 1 st, for joining in the round), placing 36 stitches on one circular needle and 37 stitches on the other circular needle. Refer to **Knitting in the round on two sets of circular needles**, on page 8, to join.

Rounds 1–8: *K2, P2, repeat from * to end of round.

Divide for the sides as follows:
Side One
Now you will begin to work in ROWS not rounds. To start working in rows, turn the work so that you are

working back across the stitches you have just made.

Row 1 (wrong side): K3, purl to last 3 stitches, K3.

Row 2: Knit to end of row.

Repeat this 2-row pattern another 16 times (18 rows in all). Leave stitches on needle. Break off yarn to darn in later.

Side Two

With the wrong side facing, join in the yarn to the stitches on other needle and work Side Two to correspond with Side One.

Upper Body

Begin working in ROUNDS again, referring to **Knitting in the round on two sets of circular needles**, on page 8.

Round 1: *K7, K2tog, repeat from * to end of round.

Round 2: Knit to end of round.

Round 3: *K6, K2tog, repeat from * to end of round.

Round 4: Knit of end of round.

Round 5: *K5, K2tog, repeat from * to end of round.

Continue in this decreasing pattern until 8 stitches remain (4 on each circular needle).

Knit one round.

Break off yarn and, with a darning needle, thread end through the remaining stitches, draw up tightly and darn in end on the wrong side.

PLASTIC BELL INSERT

The RADIUS is the most important measurement here. Measure the distance from the centre of your knitted bell to the outer fold to find the radius. Cut a plastic circle with the same radius measurement. Then cut from the outer rim to the centre of the circle and fold up to make the same shaped cone as your knitted bell. You need to insert the plastic cone into the knitted bell BEFORE you secure the edges together with masking tape or a staple or three.

PUTTING IT ALL TOGETHER

After inserting and securing the plastic cone, sew the outer cosy to the lining around the spout and handle openings. Arrange the bell to show its best side and secure with a stitch or two. If it's a hot day and your teapot needs the shade of a sombrero, gently flip the plastic insert downwards and set at a rakish Mexican angle (see page 38).

He speaks for himself. Happy green chappy.

Elfin

{Knitted cosy and lining}

SIZE
To fit a three-cup teapot that stands 9.5 cm (3¾ in) tall (not including the knob) and 14.5 cm (5¾ in) in diameter (not including the spout and handle).

MATERIALS
- 2 sets 4 mm circular needles (UK 8, US 6), 60 cm (24 in) long from needle tip to needle tip
- 3 x 50 g (1¾ oz) balls Nundle Collection 8-ply wool: Fern (see *Note*, below)
- 4 x 50 g (1¾ oz) balls Nundle Collection 8-ply wool: Lime
- Polyester fibrefill

Note. Nundle wool felts beautifully. If varying your yarn, choose 100% pure wool that felts well.

EQUIPMENT
- Darning needle
- Scissors
- Pompom maker
- Your favourite rubber gloves
- Soap

OUTER COSY

Remember! You will be working in ROUNDS and then in ROWS and things change.

Lower Body

Working from the base up, using both sets of 4 mm (UK 8, US 6) circular needles and Fern Green 8-ply wool, cast on 81 stitches (80 sts plus 1 st, for joining in the round), placing 40 stitches on one circular needle and 41 stitches on the other circular needle. Refer to **Knitting in the round on two circular needles**, on page 8, to join.

Rounds 1–10: *K2, P2, repeat from * to end of round (2 x 2 rib).

Divide for sides as follows:
Side One

Now you will begin to work in ROWS not rounds. To start working in rows, turn the work so that you are working back across the stitches you have just made.

Row 1 (wrong side): K4, purl to last 4 stitches, K4.

Row 2 (right side): Knit to end of round.

Repeat these 2 rows 9 more times, (20 rows in total, for spout and handle openings).

Leave stitches on needle. Break off yarn, leaving a long thread for darning in later.

Side Two

With wrong side facing, join in yarn to the stitches on the other needle and complete Side Two to correspond with Side One.

Upper Body

Begin working in ROUNDS again, referring to **Knitting in the round on two circular needles**, on page 8.

Rounds 1–2: Knit to end of round.

Cone decreasing pattern consists of 8 rounds: 1 decreasing round and 7 knitting rounds.

Round 3 (decreasing): *K6, K2tog, repeat from * to end of round.

Rounds 4–10: Knit to end of round.

Round 11 (decreasing): *K5, K2tog, repeat from * to end of round.

Rounds 12–18: Knit to end of round.

Round 19 (decreasing): *K4, K2tog, repeat from * to end of round.

Rounds 20–27: Knit to end of round.

Round 28 (decreasing): *K3, K2tog, repeat from * to end of round.

Rounds 29–35: Knit to end of round.

Round 36 (decreasing): *K2, K2tog, repeat from * to end of round.

Rounds: 37–43: Knit to end of round.

Round 44 (decreasing): *K1, K2tog, repeat from * to end of round.

Rounds 45–51: Knit to end of round.

Round 52 (decreasing): *K2tog, repeat from * to end of round (10 sts).

Break off yarn and, with a darning needle, thread end through remaining stitches, draw up tightly and darn in end on wrong side.

LINING

Work Lining as for Outer Cosy until decreasing rounds begin.

Dome decreasing pattern consists of 4 rounds: 1 decreasing round and 3 knitting rounds.

Round 3 (decreasing): *K2, K2tog, repeat from * to end of round.

Rounds 4–6: Knit to end of round.

Repeat these last four rows until 10 stitches remain. Break off yarn and, with a darning needle, thread end through remaining stitches, draw up tightly and darn in end on wrong side.

FELTING

Following the instructions on page 15, felt the completed cosy and lining.

POMPOMS

I bought myself some great pompom makers. I would not be without them. They are not inexpensive but you will have them forever.

Using Lime wool, I made 23 pompoms, 5 cm (2 in) diameter and 3 little pompoms, 3 cm (1¼ in) diameter. Be sure to leave a long thread on each pompom so that you are able to thread a darning needle and attach it to the outer cosy.

PUTTING IT ALL TOGETHER

Darn in all ends. Lightly stuff the cone of the outer cosy with fibrefill. The felting will help the cone stand upright quite well. Place the cone on the teapot (without the lining). Attach the pompoms evenly around the bottom approximately 2 cm (¾ in) from the lower edge. Leave space around the handle and spout for easy carrying and pouring of tea. Once the pompoms are in place, join the domed lining cosy to the inside of the outer cosy, wrong sides together, by stitching around the spout and handle openings.

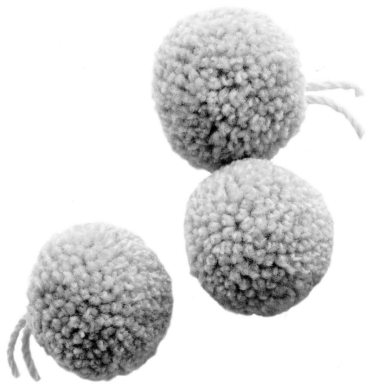

It is just granny squares. That's all.
And a little crocheted doily.
Oh, and a rose.

Nanna Deluxe

{Crocheted cosy}

SIZE
To fit a four-cup teapot that stands 14 cm (5½ in) high (not including the knob) and 14 cm (5½ in) in diameter (not including the spout and handle).

MATERIALS
- 2 x 50 g (1¾ oz) balls Jo Sharp Classic DK Wool, in 2 contrasting colours (see *Note*, below)
- 2 x 50 g (1¾ oz) balls Jo Sharp Silkroad DK Tweed, in 2 contrasting colours

Note. You will see from the photographs that I have used more than four colours, but I have the luxury of choosing from a big stash. Skite. Skite. I have suggested four colours because you need a total of four balls of wool (in weight and length) to complete the project. Feel free to raid your own stash and use extra colours.

EQUIPMENT
- 4.5 mm (UK 7, US 7) crochet hook (Granny squares)
- 4 mm (UK 8, US G/6) crochet hook (Roses)
- Darning needle
- Scissors

GRANNY SQUARES (MAKE 2 OF EACH SIZE)

Note. American crocheters, please check the Crochet Abbreviations and Conversions table on page 134.

You need to make eight Granny Squares – one set of four different sizes for each side of the cosy. Many patterns for Granny Squares add one chain stitch between each treble triplet. I prefer NOT to add that chain stitch. It makes for a much thicker, woollier fabric. And it LOOKS better without it.

Using a 4.5 mm (UK 7, US 7) hook and your colour of choice, make 5 chain. Join the chain into a circle with a slip stitch.

Round 1: 3 ch (counts as first tr), 11 tr into circle, gathering up the end thread as you go. Sl st into top of first tr (3 ch) of round. Pull end thread (gathered up in the treble stitches) tight to close circle.

Round 2: 3 ch (counts as first tr), *miss 3 tr of previous round, 6 tr into next space**, repeat from * to ** 2 more times, miss 3 tr of previous round, 5 tr, sl st into top of first 3 ch (first tr).

Round 3: 3 ch (counts as first tr), *miss 3 tr of previous round, 6 tr into next space, 3 tr into next space**, repeat from * to ** 2 more times, miss 3 tr of previous round, 5 tr, sl st into top of first 3 ch (first tr).

Continue in this same increasing pattern until your square is the desired size. The smallest Granny Square will have 6 rounds altogether. The other three sizes will have 7, 8 and 9 rounds each, respectively.

For a nice finishing edge, work one round of dc, placing 2 dc into the corners for an easy turn.

CIRCLE DOILY (MAKE 2)

Make 5 chain. Join chain into a circle with a slip stitch.

Round 1: 3 ch (counts as first tr), 11 tr into circle, gathering the loose end as you go. Sl st into top of first 3 ch (first tr) to join. Pull loose thread tight to gather in centre stitches.

Round 2: 3 ch (counts as first tr), *2 tr into space between each tr in previous round, repeat from * to last space, 1 tr into last space, sl st into top of first 3 ch to close circle.

Round 3: 3 ch (counts as first tr), *2 tr into next space, 1 tr into next space, repeat from * to last space, 1 tr into space holding first 3 ch (first tr), sl st into top of 3 ch to close circle.

Round 4: 3 ch (counts as first tr), *2 tr into next space, 1 tr into next 2 spaces, repeat from * to last space, sl st into top of 3 ch (first tr) to close circle.

Round 5: *3 ch, miss 1 tr, sl st into next tr, repeat from * to end.

Cut yarn and darn into back of work.

ROSES (MAKE 2)

Following the instructions on page 123, make 2 crocheted roses.

LOWER BAND

Using a sturdy 8-ply wool make 60 chain. Join in a circle with a slip stitch. Work 4 rounds of dc. Sl st to finish off.

MINI GRANNY SQUARES

To cover the Lower Band under the spout and handle, make 4 mini Granny Squares, two for the spout and two for the handle. Each mini Granny Square will be two rounds wide.

PUTTING IT ALL TOGETHER

Darn in all ends. Layer the Granny Squares in two matching piles, from largest to smallest, with a Circle Doily and a Rose on top, and stitch together at key points. Pin the cosy parts in place on the teapot for a perfect fit before stitching the two top corners of each pile together, to join. Stitch the Lower Band around the inside of the lower edge of the cosy and stitch two mini Granny Squares on the Lower Band below each opening.

Still Life

{Knitted cosy, flowers and tray}

SIZE

To fit a three-cup teapot that stands 10 cm (4 in) tall (not including the knob) and 13 cm (5 in) in diameter (not including the spout and handle).

MATERIALS

- 2 x 50 g (1¾ oz) balls Noro Silk Garden (see *Note*, below)
- 1 x 50 g (1¾ oz) ball 8-ply yarn, in a contrasting colour
- One handful polyester fibrefill

Note. Noro Silk Garden comes in many beautiful shades. You are best to choose your favourite colour from your nearest yummy craft store, or on-line.

EQUIPMENT

- Two sets 4 mm (UK 8, US 6) circular needles, 60 cm (24 in) long from needle tip to needle tip
- Scissors
- Darning needle

BODY AND LINING

The cosy and lining are worked in one piece, which is then folded in on itself to create the lining. The Body is knitted in Bramble stitch, which is worked on a multiple of 4 stitches over 4 rows.

Remember! You will be working in ROUNDS and then in ROWS and things change.

Lower Body

Using both sets of 4 mm (UK 8, US 6) circular needles and Noro Silk Garden yarn, cast on 65 stitches (64 sts plus 1 st, for joining in the round), placing 32 stitches on one circular needle and 33 stitches on the other circular needle. Refer to **Knitting in the round on two sets of circular needles**, on page 8, to join.

Round 1: Knit to end of round.
Round 2: *(K1, P1, K1) into next st, P3tog, repeat from * to end of round.
Round 3: Knit to end of round.
Round 4: *P3tog, (K1, P1, K1) into next st, repeat from * to end of round.

Last 4 rounds form Bramble stitch pattern.

Round 5: Knit to end of round.

Round 6: *(K1, P1, K1) into next st, P3tog, repeat from * to end of round.

Divide for sides as follows:

Side One

Now you will begin to work in ROWS not rounds. To start working in rows, turn the work so that you are working back across the stitches you have just made, keeping the Bramble stitch pattern correct.

Row 7 (right side): Purl to end of row.

Row 8 (wrong side): *(K1, P1, K1) into next st, P3tog, repeat from * to end of row.

Row 9: Purl to end of row.

Row 10: *P3tog, (K1, P1, K1) into next st, repeat from * to end of row.

Repeat the last 4 rows three more times (or until the knitted work reaches to the top of your tea pot handle.

Row 23: Purl to end of row.

Row 24: *(K1, P1, K1) into next st, P3tog, repeat from * to end of row.

Leave these stitches on needle. Break off yarn, leaving a long length to darn in later.

Side Two

With the right side facing you, (right side is raised bobble texture), join yarn to first stitch on the other circular needles and work Side Two to correspond with Side One.

Upper Body

Referring to **Knitting in the round on two circular needles**, on page 8, join the two sides together into a round again and continue in Bramble stitch pattern as follows:

(Note. Check that the instructions in the following rounds look like the right thing to do next to keep your Bramble stitch pattern correct. Trust your understanding of the pattern and follow your instinct, especially if you have added rows for a larger teapot.)

Round 25: Knit to end of round

Round 26: *P3tog, (K1, P1, K1) into next st, repeat from * to end of round.

Round 27: Knit to end of round.

Round 28: *(K1, P1, K1) into next st, P3tog, repeat from * to end of round.

Repeat these 4 rounds twice more.

Round 37: Knit to end of row.

Round 38: *P3tog; (K1, P1, K1) into next st, repeat from * to end of round.

(DO NOT cast off.)

LINING

Change to the contrasting 8-ply yarn.

Upper Body

Round 39: *K1, P1, repeat from * to end of round.

Round 40: *K1, P1, repeat from * to end of round (1x1 rib).

Repeat these 2 rounds five more times (12 rounds of ribbing in total).

Divide for sides as follows:

Side One

Now you will begin to work in ROWS not rounds. To start working in rows, turn the work so that you are working back across the stitches you have just made. Work Side One in 1x1 rib for 18 rows.

Leave these stitches on needle. Break off yarn, leaving a tail to darn in later.

Side Two

Join yarn to the stitches on the other needle and work 18 rows of 1x1 rib to correspond with Side One.

Lower Body

Referring to **Knitting in the round on two circular needles**, on page 8, join the two sides together into a ROUND again. Continue in 1x1 rib for 5 rounds. Cast off loosely.

ROSES (MAKE 8 OR 9)

Amazingly, the length of yarn required to make one flower is almost exactly the length of yarn from colour change to colour change in the Noro Silk Garden range. Following the instructions on page 118, make 8 or 9 knitted roses.

ROSE TRAY (MAKE 1 OR 2)

If your teapot lid is flat, you can give your roses some lovely height by making two trays. Lay the trays, one on top of the other like pancakes, sew the edges together and stuff with a little polyester fibrefill.

Your roses will look as if they are sitting in a vase, as fresh as the day is new.

Using both sets of 4 mm (UK 8, US 6) circular needles and contrasting 8-ply yarn, cast on 15 stitches (14 sts plus 1 st, for joining in the round), placing 7 stitches on one circular needle and 8 stitches on the other circular needle. Refer to **Knitting in the round on two circular needles**, on page 8, to join.

Round 1: Knit to end of round.
Round 2: *K1, increase once in next stitch, repeat from * to end of round.
Round 3 (and each alternate round): Knit to end of round.

Round 4: *K2, increase once in next stitch, repeat from * to end of round.
Round 6: *K3, increase once in next stitch, repeat from * to end of round.
Round 8: *K4, increase once in next stitch, repeat from * to end of round.
Round 10: *K5, increase once in next stitch, repeat from * to end of round.
Round 12: *K6, increase once in next stitch, repeat from * to end of round.
Round 14: *K7, increase once in next stitch, repeat from * to end of round.
Round 16: *K8, increase once in next stitch, repeat from * to end of round.
Round 17: Knit to end of round.

Before you cast off, try it on your teapot, with the sock body, for size. If it is not quite big enough, continue in the increasing pattern until it is the desired size. Cast off.

PUTTING IT ALL TOGETHER

Darn in all ends. Fold the tea cosy sock in on itself, aligning the openings for the spout and handle. Sew the lining and the outer sock together at the edges of the spout opening and handle opening.

Place the tea cosy over the teapot with the folded edge at the top. Pin the tray into place and sew into position, securing it to both the inner and outer sock walls.

Arrange the roses on the tray and sew each item firmly into place. Keep checking that the arrangement is falling into place as you attach each item.

The Manx Loaghtan wool travelled all the way from the Isle of Man with a friend. Just two balls. The wool is not soft or pretty, but I was so chuffed with the gift for the gift's sake, that I was determined to use it well. And so Beauty and the Beast was born and immortalised in my first book, *Wild Tea Cosies*. A stranger loved the original cosy a little too well and stole it from a bookstore while on display there. I didn't mourn the loss of my cosy as much as I did the loss of Merryn's gift. So off Merryn went again to the Isle of Man, just to get me two more balls of Manx Loaghtan wool, and in a snap – Modern Primitive.

Modern Primitive

{Knitted cosy; crocheted decoration}

SIZE
To fit a four-cup teapot that stands 13 cm (5 in) tall (not including the knob) and 12 cm (4¾ in) in diameter (not including the spout and handle).

MATERIALS
- 2 x 50 g (1¾ oz) balls Pure Manx Loaghtan Aran (12-ply) Wool (Outer Cosy)
- 1 x 50 g (1¾ oz) ball Nundle Collection 8-ply wool: Brown (Lining)
- For the Eyes, Fringe Skirt and Topknot, use up all the colours of your stash. If you want it to look exactly like mine, use Noro Kureyon sock wool for the Eyes and Noro Kureyon for the Fringe Skirt
- Polyester fibrefill

EQUIPMENT
- Two sets 5 mm (UK 6, US 8) circular needles, 60 cm (24 in) long from needle tip to needle tip (Outer Cosy)
- Two sets 4 mm (UK 8, US 6) circular needles, 60 cm (24 in) long from needle tip to needle tip (Lining)
- 3 mm (UK 11, US D/3) crochet hook (Eyes)
- Darning needle
- Scissors

OUTER COSY

Remember! You will be working in ROUNDS and then in ROWS and things change.

Lower Body

Working from the lower edge up, using both sets of 5 mm (UK 6, US 8) circular needles and Manx Loaghtan wool, cast on 81 stitches (80 sts plus 1 st, for joining in the round), placing 40 stitches on one circular needle and 41 stitches on the other circular needle. Refer to **Knitting in the round on two sets of circular needles**, on page 8, to join.

Rounds 1–10: *K2, P2, repeat from * to end of round (2x2 rib).

Divide for sides as follows:
Side One

Now you will begin to work in ROWS not rounds. To start working in rows, turn the work so that you are working back across the stitches you have just made. Work 20 rows in garter stitch. (To make garter stitch while working in ROWS, knit every row.)

Side Two

Join the yarn to Side Two and complete to correspond with Side One.

Upper Body

Referring to **Knitting in the round on two sets of circular needles**, on page 8, begin working in ROUNDS again with the wrong side facing. (When the decreasing and looping pattern is finished, you will turn the cosy inside out so that the loops and the 'wrong' side of the stocking stitch are facing outwards.)

To 'make loop'

Insert needle into next stitch, wind yarn over the needle point, then over one finger of the left hand and over the needle point again. Draw the 2 loops through the stitch and place them back on the left needle. Knit through the back of the two loops.

Rounds 1 and 2: Knit to end of round.

Now the 4-round decreasing pattern begins. Feel the rhythm. It goes like this: loop round; knit round; loop round; decrease round.

Round 3: *'make loop', K18, 'make loop', repeat from * to end of round.

Round 4: Knit to end of round.

Round 5: *'make loop', K18, 'make loop', repeat from * to end of round.

Round 6: *K18, K2tog, repeat from * to end of round.

Round 7: *'make loop', K17, 'make loop', repeat from * to end of round.

Round 8: Knit to end of round.

Round 9: *'make loop', K17, 'make loops', repeat from * to end of round.

Round 10: *K17, K2tog, repeat from * to end of round.

Round 11: *'make loop', K16, 'make loop', repeat from * to end of round.

Round 12: Knit to end of round.

Round 13: *'make loop', K16, 'make loop', repeat from * to end of round.

Round 14: *K16, K2tog, repeat from * to end of round.

Round 15: *'make loop', K15, 'make loop', repeat from * to end of round.

Round 16: Knit to end of round.

Round 17: *'make loop', K15, 'make loop', repeat from * to end of round.

Round 18: *K15, K2tog, repeat from * to end of round.

Round 19: *'make loop', K14, 'make loop', repeat from * to end of round.

Round 20: Knit to end of round.

Round 21: *'make loop', K14, 'make loop', repeat from *

to end of round.

Round 22: *K14, K2tog, repeat from * to end of round.

Round 23: *'make loop', K13, 'make loop', repeat from * to end of round.

Round 24: Knit to end of round.

Round 25: *'make loop', K13, 'make loop', repeat from * to end of round.

Round 26: *K13, K2tog, repeat from * to end of round.

Round 27: *'make loop', K12, 'make loop', repeat from * to end of round.

Round 28: Knit to end of round.

Round 29: *'make loop', K12, 'make loop', repeat from * to end of round.

Round 30: *K12, K2tog, repeat from * to end of round.

Round 31: *'make loop', K11, 'make loop', repeat from * to end of round.

Round 32: Knit to end of round.

Round 33: *'make loop', K11, 'make loop', repeat from * to end of round.

Round 34: *K11, K2tog, repeat from * to end of round.

Round 35: *'make loop', K10, 'make loop', repeat from * to end of round.

Round 36: Knit to end of round.

Round 37: *'make loop', K10, 'make loop', repeat from * to end of round.

Round 38: *K10, K2tog, repeat from * to end of round.

Round 39: *'make loop', K9, 'make loop', repeat from * to end of round.

Round 40: Knit to end of round.

Round 41: *'make loop', K9, 'make loop', repeat from * to end of round.

Round 42: *K9, K2tog, repeat from * to end of round.

Round 43: *'make loop', K8, 'make loop', repeat from * to end of round.

Round 44: Knit to end of round.

Round 45: *'make loop', K8, 'make loop', repeat from * to end of round.

Round 46: *K8, K2tog, repeat from * to end of round.

Flat top

Round 47: Knit to end of round.

Round 48: *K7, K2tog, repeat from * to end of round.

Round 49: *K6, K2tog, repeat from * to end of round.

Round 50: *K5, K2tog, repeat from * to end of round.

Round 51: *K4, K2tog, repeat from * to end of round.

Round 52: *K3, K2tog, repeat from * to end of round.

Round 53: *K2, K2tog, repeat from * to end of round.

Round 54: *K1, K2tog, repeat from * to end of round.

Round 55: K2tog to end of round.

Cut the yarn and, with a darning needle, thread the end through the remaining stitches and pull up tightly to close.

LINING

Lower Body

Using both sets of 4 mm (UK 8, US 6) circular needles and Brown 8-ply wool, cast on 81 stitches (80 sts plus 1 st, for joining in the round), placing 40 stitches on one circular needle and 41 stitches on the other circular needle. Refer to **Knitting in the round on two sets of circular needles**, on page 8, to join.

Rounds 1–10: *K2, P2, repeat from * to end of round (2x2 rib).

Divide for sides as follows:

Side One

Now you will begin to work in ROWS not rounds. To start working in rows, turn the work so that you are working back across the stitches you have just made.

Row 1 (wrong side): K4, purl to last 4 sts, K4.

Row 2 (right side): Knit to end of row.

Repeat these 2 rows 12 more times (26 rows in all, for spout and handle openings).

Break off yarn, leaving a long thread for darning in later.

Side Two

With wrong side of work facing, join in the yarn to

the stitches on the other needle and work Side Two to correspond with Side One.

Crown

Begin working in rounds again, referring to **Knitting in the round on two sets of circular needles**, on page 8.

Rounds 1–4: Knit to end of round.

Round 5: *K8, K2tog, repeat from * to end of round.

Round 6: Knit to end of round.

Round 7: *K7, K2tog, repeat from * to end of round.

Round 8: Knit to end of round.

Round 9: *K6, K2tog, repeat from * to end of round.

Round 10: Knit to end of round.

Continue in this decreasing pattern until 8 stitches remain.

Break off yarn and, with a darning needle, thread the end through remaining stitches, pull up tightly to close and darn in end on wrong side.

EYES

Note. American crocheters, please check the Crochet Abbreviations and Conversions table on page 134.

You'll need two contrasting colours to get a spiral effect. Using a 3 mm (UK 11, US D/3) crochet hook and Noro Kureyon sock wool (or any 4-ply wool), make 4 chain. Join the chain into a circle with a slip stitch.

Round 1: Make 2 ch (counts as first dc), 7 dc into circle.

Round 2: *2 dc into first dc (2 ch), 1dc into next dc, repeat from * to end of round.

Mark the beginning of each round with a short piece of contrasting coloured thread.

Round 3: Add in the contrasting colour at the beginning of the round with a slip stitch and 2ch (counts as 1st dc of contrasting colour). *2 dc into first dc, 1 dc into next 2 dc, repeat from * to end of round.

Round 4: *2 dc into first dc, 1 dc into next 3 dc, repeat from * to end of round.

Continue working in the round with one colour chasing the other colour, increasing in this fashion and checking often that you are producing a flat doily. If the crocheted fabric is too cone-like, then you need to increase more often. If the crocheted fabric is buckling up like a wavy frill, you need to increase less often.

When the circle has reached the desired size, end each of the two coloured yarns in a slip stitch and darn into the back of the work.

PUTTING IT ALL TOGETHER

Darn in all ends. Turn the outer cone inside out so that the loops and the 'wrong' side of the stocking stitch are now on the outside. Using matching thread, stitch the Eyes to the front (that is, the spout) side of the cosy.

Now gather up all your bits and pieces of scrap wool to make the Fringe Skirt and Topknot. Cut lots and lots and lots of bits of wool, about 15 cm (6 in) long. Don't be slavish about getting the length exact every time – it is 'primitive', remember, and 'modern'. Working on the right side of the outer cosy and starting about 3 cm (1¼ in) above the lower edge, push your crochet hook through the knitted fabric, pick up the loop on a doubled length of wool, draw it through the knitted fabric, then pull the ends through the loop and pull firmly to knot it in place. Work your way around the bottom section of the cosy adding the fringe in this way, until you have covered the area below the loops – or gone insane (whichever happens first).

Take a deep breath (you're nearly there) and fill in the flat top thickly in the same way, to create the Topknot.

Lightly stuff the cone with fibrefill. With wrong sides together, attach the outer cosy to the lining round the spout and handle openings.

It must be tea time!

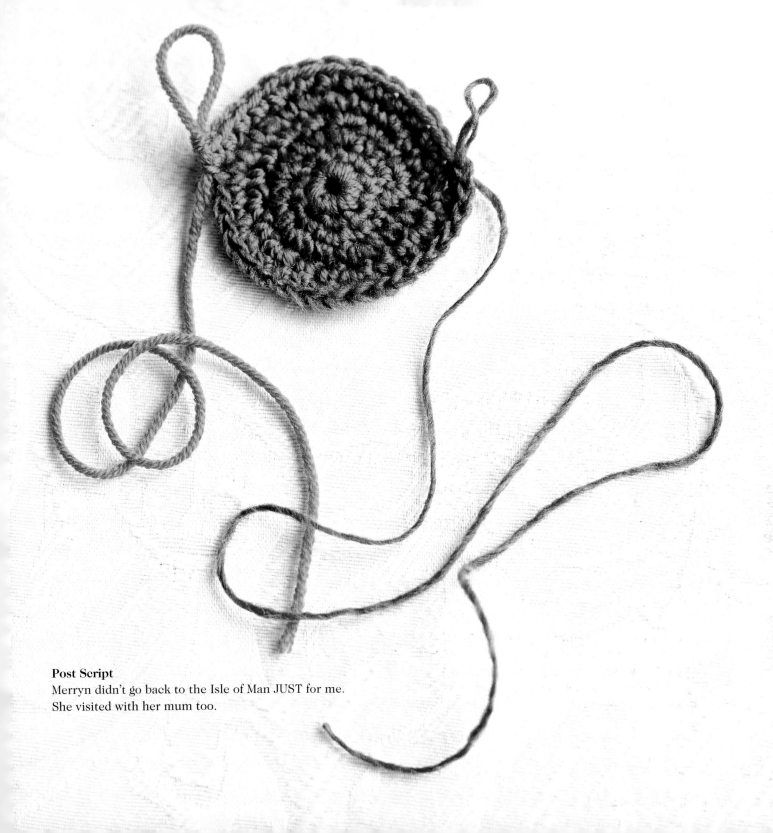

Post Script
Merryn didn't go back to the Isle of Man JUST for me.
She visited with her mum too.

I named this little beauty 'Grecian Lovely' but when I put the feathers in at the last, I wanted to put it on my head and trot off to the races. Ah! So many possibilities.

Grecian Lovely
{Knitted tea cosy}

SIZE
To fit a two-cup teapot that stands 9 cm (3½ in) tall (not including the knob) and 12 cm (4¾ in) in diameter (not including the spout and handle).

MATERIALS
- 1 x 50 g (1¾ oz) ball Nundle Collection 8-ply wool, Main Colour (MC): Black
- 1 x 50 g (1¾ oz) ball Nundle Collection 8-ply wool, Contrasting Colour (CC): Amethyst
- Polyester fibrefill
- Feathers

EQUIPMENT
- Two sets 4 mm (UK 8, US 6) circular needles, 60 cm (24 in) long from needle tip to needle tip
- Scissors
- Darning needle

BODY

Lower Body

Remember! You will be working in ROUNDS and then in ROWS and things change.

Using both sets of 4 mm (UK 8, US 6) circular needles and MC, cast on 81 stitches (80 sts plus 1 st, for joining in the round), placing 40 stitches on one circular needle and 41 stitches on the other circular needle. Refer to **Knitting in the round on two sets of circular needles,** on page 8, to join.

Round 1: *K2, P2, repeat from * to end of round (2x2 rib).
Round 2: Join in CC, *K2 (MC), P2 (CC), repeat from * to end of round, carrying the threads loosely across the back of the work, leaving room for elasticity in the finished knitted fabric.
Continue the striped rib pattern for 5 more rounds.

Divide for sides as follows:
Side One

Now you will begin to work in ROWS not rounds. To start working in rows, turn the work so that you are working back across the stitches you have just made.
Working in ROWS, continue the striped ribbed stitch pattern up first side of tea cosy for 18 rows.
Leave stitches on needle. Break off yarn, leaving a long length to darn in later.

Side Two

With the wrong side facing you, join the yarn to the first stitch on the other circular needles and knit Side Two to correspond to Side One.
Break off the CC yarn to darn in later.

Upper Body

Referring to **Knitting in the round on two sets of circular needles**, on page 8, begin working in ROUNDS again with the right facing, using MC only.

Round 1: *K2, P2tog, repeat from * to end of round.
Round 2: * K2, P1, repeat from * to end of round.
Continue in the K2, P1 ribbing pattern for a further 20 rounds. Join in CC.
Round 23: *K2 (MC), K1 (CC), repeat from * to end of round, carrying yarn loosely, as before.
Round 24: *K2 (MC), increase once in next st using CC, repeat from * to end of round.
Round 25: *K2 (MC), P2 (CC), repeat from * to end of round.
Continue in the striped ribbing pattern for a further 4 rounds.

Lid

Break off MC yarn to darn in later.
To give the clever folding effect at the top of the cosy, reverse the ribbing pattern by purling the knit stitches and knitting the purl stitches, thus (working in CC only):

Rounds 30–35: *P2, K2, repeat from * to end of round.
Round 36: *P2, K2tog, repeat from * to end of round.
Rounds 37–42: *P2, K1, repeat from * to end of round.
Round 43: *P2tog, K1, repeat from * to end of round.
Rounds 44–46: *P1, K1, repeat from * to end of round.
Round 47: K2tog to end of round.
Rounds 48–50: Knit to end of round.
Break off yarn and, with a darning needle, thread end through remaining stitches, draw up tightly and darn in end on the wrong side.

LINING

Lower Body

Using both sets of 4 mm (UK 8, US 6) circular needles and MC, cast on 69 stitches (68 sts plus 1 st, for joining in the round), placing 34 stitches on one circular needle and 35 stitches on the other circular needle. Refer to **Knitting in the round on two circular needles**, on page 8, to join.

Rounds 1–5: *K2, P2, repeat from * to end of round (2x2 rib).

Divide for sides as follows:

Side One
Now you will begin to work in ROWS not rounds. To start working in rows, turn the work so that you are working back across the stitches you have just made.
Row 1 (wrong side): K3, purl to last 3 sts, K3.
Row 2: Knit to end of row.
Repeat these 2 rows 8 more times (18 rows in all, for spout and handle openings).
Leave stitches on needle. Break off yarn, leaving a long thread for darning in later.

Side Two
With wrong side facing, join in yarn to the stitches on the other needle and work Side Two to correspond with Side One.

Crown
Begin working in rounds again, referring to **Knitting in the round on two circular needles**, on page 8.
Round 1: *K8, K2tog, repeat from * to end of round.
Round 2: Knit to end of round.
Round 3: *K7, K2tog, repeat from * to end of round.
Round 4: Knit to end of round.
Round 5: *K6, K2tog, repeat from * to end of round.
Continue in this decreasing pattern until 8 stitches remain (4 on each circular needle).
Knit one round.
Break off yarn and, with a darning needle, thread end through remaining stitches, pull up tightly to close and darn in end on the wrong side.

PUTTING IT ALL TOGETHER
Darn in all ends. Loosely fill the stem of the vessel with fibrefill. Place the lining inside the outer cosy, with wrong sides together and spout and handle holes aligned. Sew the inner and outer teapot garments together around the edges of the spout and handle holes and around the crown of the lining, ensuring that your stitches are not visible on the outer cosy. Sew a flourish of feathers inside the top of the cosy, taking the thread down through the centre to the inside of the centre top of the lining to secure everything in place nicely.

Loopy Lou needs to be taken to its final felted conclusion to realise her true fantastic fabulousness.

Loopy Lou
{Knitted}

SIZE
To fit a three-cup teapot that stands 11 cm (4¼ in) tall (not including the knob) and 14.5cm (5¾ in) in diameter (not including the spout and handle).

MATERIALS
- 2 x 50 g (1¾ oz) balls Nundle Collection 8-ply wool: Blue (see *Note*, below)
- 6 contrasting colours for the loops from your stash (preferably good felting wool)

Note. Nundle wool felts beautifully. If varying your yarn, choose 100% pure wool that felts well.

EQUIPMENT
- Two sets 4 mm (UK 8, US 6) circular needles, 60 cm (24 in) long from needle tip to needle tip
- One pair 4 mm (UK 8, US 6) double-pointed needles (for loops)
- Darning needle
- Scissors
- Your favourite rubber gloves
- Soap

COSY/LINING (MAKE 2)

How about this for easy? The Cosy and lining are exactly the same – unless you want to make them in different colours. It is not essential that you make a lining for Loopy Lou, but I really do think that a lining makes all the difference. A tea cosy with a lining makes it more perky, helps it last longer and, the all-essential one, keeps the tea piping hot.

Lower Body

Remember! You will be working in ROUNDS and then in ROWS and things change.

Using both sets of 4 mm (UK 8, US 6) circular needles and 8-ply Blue, cast on 73 stitches (72 sts plus 1 st, for joining in the round), placing 36 stitches on one circular needle and 37 stitches on the other circular needle. Refer to **Knitting in the round on two sets of circular needles**, on page 8, to join.

Round 1: *K1, P1, repeat from * to end of round.
Round 2: *P1, K1, repeat from * to end of round.
Round 3: *K1, P1, repeat from * to end of round.
Rounds 4–9: Knit to end of round.

Divide for sides as follows:

Side One

Now you will begin to work in ROWS not rounds. To start working in rows, turn the work so that you are working back across the stitches you have just made.
Row 1 (wrong side): K1, P1, K1, purl to last 3 stitches, K1, P1, K1.
Row 2: K1, P1, knit to last 2 stitches, P1, K1.
Rows 3–22: Keeping the moss stitch edges correct, as before, continue in stocking stitch.
Leave stitches on needle. Break off yarn, leaving a length to darn in later.

Side Two

With the wrong side facing you, join the yarn to the first stitch on the other circular needles and knit Side Two to correspond to Side One.

Upper Body

Referring to **Knitting in the round on two sets of circular needles**, on page 8, begin working in ROUNDS again as follows:
Round 1 (and each alternate round): Knit to end of round.
Round 2: *K7, K2tog, repeat from * to end of round.
Round 4: *K6, K2tog, repeat from * to end of round.
Round 6: *K5, K2tog, repeat from * to end of round.
Continue in this decreasing pattern until 8 stitches remain (4 on each circular needle). Break off yarn and, with a darning needle, thread end through remaining 8 stitches, draw up tightly and darn in end on wrong side.

I-cords

Following the I-cord instructions on page 129, make about 23 x 20 cm (8 in) lengths in a rainbow of colours, leaving a tail of thread extending at each end.

PUTTING IT ALL TOGETHER

Stitch the I-cord loops randomly over the surface of the outer cosy, using the tail threads to anchor them firmly. With wrong sides together, sew the outer and inner cosies together around the handle and spout openings, with a couple of extra stitches at odd points around the base.

FELTING

Referring to the instructions on page 15, felt the completed tea cosy.

Champion Chooks

The next two tea cosies are a couple of champion chooks. You might be wondering what on earth a 'chook' is. The dictionary definition reads:

chook n. Aust. 1 a chicken or fowl. 2 colloq. an older woman. Running about like a headless chook colloq: acting in a panic-stricken manner and not thinking clearly about what should be done.

But we shouldn't ignore...

Braaak: the sound a chook makes, still in possession of its head.

Clever Chook: a person of intelligence (or a chook still in possession of its head).

That covers just about everything, from the sublime to the ridiculous.

Introducing **Roger Rampant** and **Pedro de la Pantaloon**. Yes yes. Not very Australian. Forgive them. These are their stage names. Everybody is a comedian.

Roger LOOKS tricky to make but if you can knit a stitch and purl a stitch and if you can crochet a double chain stitch, you can make Roger Rampant. No two Roger Rampants will be the same.

Oh yes! He boasts a peg collection to die for. I know. I know. Who'd have thought a PEG collection, with a name like that? I understand he is partial to a game of *boules* every now and then too. And the odd nip of brandy with his tea.

Roger Rampant

(spoken with a French Accent)

{Knitted and crocheted}

SIZE
I made him to fit a two-cup teapot that stands 9 cm (3½ in) tall (not including the knob) and 12 cm (4¾ in) in diameter (not including the spout and handle).

MATERIALS
- 2 x 50 g (1¾ oz) balls Noro Kureyon (choose two different but complementary colours)
- 1 x 50 g (1¾ oz) ball Nundle Collection 8-ply wool: Red
- A very small amount of Yellow Nundle Collection 8-ply wool
- Bonsai wire, twice the length you want for the neck
- 2 large (3 cm/1¼ in) buttons with 4 sewing holes (not 2 sewing holes) in each

EQUIPMENT
- 5 mm (UK 6, US H/8) crochet hook
- Two sets 4 mm (UK 8, US 6) circular needles, 60 cm (24 in) long from needle tip to needle tip
- One pair 5 mm (UK 6, US 8) double-pointed needles
- One pair 4 mm (UK 8, US 6) double-pointed needles
- Darning needle
- Scissors

Note: American crocheters, please check the Crochet Abbreviations and Conversions table on page 134.

BODY

Feather Tendrils

Begin by winding some of the Noro Kureyon into smaller balls of wool, length defined by the colour change.

Using a 5 mm (UK6, US H/8) hook and one of your small balls of Noro Kureyon wool, make 5 chain. Sl st into first chain to close the circle. Make 2 ch (counts as first dc). Make 8 dc into the circle, join with a sl st to first st. Continue working in the round until desired length. There are three general sizes: small, medium and large, the largest being as long as my index finger.

When you have five or six tendrils of different sizes (about 18–20 tendrils in all), sew them together at the base, forming a neat circle. The first three or four tendrils might be a bit fiddly, but it gets easier and easier as it grows. Don't be too precious about it. It will all work out beautifully in the end. Note though, how most of the larger tendrils are placed towards the handle end of the teapot where the larger feathers on a rooster grow.

Crochet binding

Place the feather tendril circle on top of the teapot to test for size. When you are happy that the circle is big enough, bind it all together around the outer edge with a round of dc stitch, using the 5 mm (UK6, US H/8) hook and Noro Kureyon yarn, and gathering the tendril edges into as much of a uniformly curved edge as possible. Mark the beginning of the next round with a short thread of contrasting wool. Continue to work dc for one more round, counting the stitches as you go. Slip stitch in the next dc and tie off.

Body Sides (knitted)

Divide the total number of dcs in the round by two. I counted 52 dcs on mine (26 plus 26 stitches). You might have a few more stitches or several fewer. It doesn't matter.

Side One

Using one set of 4 mm (UK 8, US 6) circular knitting needles and Noro Kureyon wool, and with the right side facing, pick up 26 (or thereabouts) stitches to begin knitting the first side. Whatever number of stitches you have there now (on one side) needs to be turned into 40 knitted stitches by the end of the first row. You can do this with a little bit of primary school maths. The important number to be going on with is 40.

I had to turn 26 picked-up stitches into 40 knitted stitches. I did it like this: 40 minus 26 equals 14. I needed to increase 14 times (reasonably) evenly across the side. To increase, knit into the front and back of the same stitch.

At the end of this row of stitches (it should now be 40), turn and K2, P2 to end of row. You have now set up the 2x2 ribbed pattern. Continue for 20 rows rib (in total) or until the side measures to just under the spout and handle. Leave stitches on needle and break off yarn.

Side Two

Join in yarn and, using the second set of 4 mm (UK 8, US 6) circular needles, work Side Two to correspond to Side One.

Lower Body

Referring to **Knitting in the round on two sets of circular needles**, on page 8, join the two sides together into a round again and continue in 2x2 ribbed pattern for 8 rounds.

Cast off loosely.

HEAD AND NECK

Neck I-cord

Using the 5 mm (UK 6, US 8) double-pointed needles and two strands of Yellow wool, cast on 4 stitches. *Slide the stitches to the other end of the needle. Take the yarn across the back of the work from left to right and knit the four stitches**. Repeat from * to ** until I-cord measures 5 cm (2 in). Change to two strands of Noro Kureyon and continue the I-cord for a further 30 cm (12 in), or neck measurement of your fancy. Cast off.

Comb and Wattle I-cord (make 2 lengths)

Using the 4 mm (UK 8, US 6) double-pointed needles and one strand of Red wool, cast on 4 stitches. Follow the instructions for the Neck I-cord, above, to make two 20 cm (8 in) lengths of I-cord.

LINING

The lining is essential. It will give weight to the base of the cosy and protect the teapot from the bonsai wire.

Lower Body

Using both sets of 4 mm (UK 8, US 6) circular needles and Red, cast on 73 stitches (72 sts plus 1 st, for joining in the round), placing 36 stitches on one circular needle and 37 stitches on the other circular needle. Refer to **Knitting in the round on two sets of circular needles**, on page 8, to join.

Rounds 1–8: *K2, P2, repeat from * to end of round (2x2 rib).

Divide for sides as follows:

Side One

Now you will begin to work in ROWS not rounds. To start working in rows, turn the work so that you are working back across the stitches you have just made.

Row 1 (wrong side): K3, purl to last 3 stitches, K3.

Row 2: Knit to end of row.

Repeat this two-row pattern until you have completed 18 rows for Side One.
Leave stitches on needle. Break off yarn to darn in later.

Side Two
With wrong side facing, join in the yarn to stitches on other needle and work Side Two to correspond with Side One.

Upper Body
Referring to **Knitting in the round on two sets of circular needles**, on page 8, begin working in ROUNDS again as follows:

Round 1: *K7, K2tog, repeat from * to end of round.
Round 2: Knit to end of round.
Round 3: *K6, K2tog, repeat from * to end of round.
Round 4: Knit to end of round.
Round 5: *K5, K2tog, repeat from * to end of round.
Continue in this decreasing pattern until 8 stitches remain (4 on each circular needle).
Knit one round.
Break off yarn and, with a darning needle, thread end through the remaining stitches, draw up tightly and darn in end on the wrong side.

PUTTING IT ALL TOGETHER
Darn in all ends. Cut a bonsai wire long enough to thread through the skinny neck I-cord, with enough extra wire to coil in a circle under the Feather Tendrils. Loop the bonsai wire back on itself at one end for safety and for ease of threading. The loop must be small enough to be able to thread up through the centre of the I-cord. Thread the bonsai wire up through the head and neck I-cord. With yellow yarn, sew the beak to the end loop of the inserted wire. (This is to stop the wire from slipping back out of the I-cord.) Stretch the I-cord down over the wire. You should have approximately 20 cm (8 in) of extending wire to play with at the end.
You need to make another loop in the wire at this point

to attach the I-cord to, but BEFORE YOU DO, poke the remaining wire down through the crocheted Feather Tendrils of the body to the underside of the cosy along with the yarn end of the neck I-cord. Bend a loop in the wire and wrap and knot the yarn end tightly around the loop to keep the I-cord from riding back up the wire. Now that you have secured the end of the neck I-cord, curve the remaining wire in a wide circle and stitch into place to the underside of the Feather Tendrils.

Now back to the rooster's head … Loop the wattle I-cord into two equal loops and stitch into place below the beak. Loop the comb I-cord into 3 equal loops and stitch into place on the head. Sew on the button eyes.
With wrong sides together, put the lining inside the cosy and stitch the lining into place around the openings for the spout and handle, adding two or three stitches on the bottom edge of either side.
Bend that scrawny old neck into shape.

Ah Pedro, you little beauty. Walks along the beach at sunset?
Dinner by candlelight? Poetic romancing? Poker? I'm yours, baby.
I'm yours.

Pedro de la Pantaloon

{Knitted}

SIZE
To fit a three-cup teapot that stands 9.5 cm (3¾ in) tall (not including the
knob) and 14.5 cm (5¾ in) in diameter (not including the spout and handle).

MATERIALS
- 1 x 50 g (1¾ oz) ball Noro Kureyon (colour of your own choosing)
- 2 x 50 g (1¾ oz) balls Nundle Collection 8-ply wool: Periwinkle
- 1 x 50 g (1¾ oz) ball Nundle Collection 8-ply wool: Red
- Small amount Nundle Collection 8-ply wool: Yellow
- Small amount black yarn, for sewing eyes
- Polyester fibrefill
- 2 large (5 cm/2 in) red buttons
- Fabulous feathers
- Thin cardboard, to make a cone shape

EQUIPMENT
- Two sets 4 mm (UK 8, US 6) circular needles, 60 cm long from needle
  tip to needle tip
- Three x 4 mm (UK 8, US 6) double-pointed needles
- Darning needle
- Scissors

CONE NECK

The neck is knitted from the beak down.

Using both sets of 4 mm (UK 8, US 6) circular needles and Yellow, cast on 7 stitches (6 sts plus 1 st, for joining in the round), placing 3 stitches on one circular needle and 4 stitches on the other circular needle. Refer to **Knitting in the round on two sets of circular needles,** on page 8.

Rounds 1–4: Knit to end of round.

Round 5: Knit to end of round, increasing once in the 1st and 4th stitches (8 sts).

Rounds 6–8: Knit to end of round.

Round 9: Knit to end of round, increasing once in the 1st and 5th stitches (10 sts).

Rounds 10–12: Knit to end of round.

Round 13: Knit to end of round, increasing once in the 1st and 6th stitches (12 sts).

Round 14: Knit to end of round.

Change to Noro Kureyon.

Round 15 and 16: Knit to end of round.

Round 17: *Increase once in next stitch, K1, repeat from * to end of round.

Rounds 18–22: Knit to end of round.

Round 23: *Increase once in next stitch, K2, repeat from * to end of round.

Rounds 24–28: Knit to end of round.

Round 29: *Increase once in next stitch, K3, repeat from * to end of round.

Rounds 30–34: Knit to end of round.

Round 35: *Increase once in next stitch, K4, repeat from * to end of round.

Rounds 36–40: Knit to end of round.

Round 41: *Increase once in next stitch, K5, repeat from * to end of round.

Rounds 42–46: Knit to end of round.

Round 47: *Increase once in next stitch, K6, repeat from * to end of round.

Rounds 48–50: Knit to end of round (noting that this is 3 rounds not 5 rounds as previously).

Round 51: *Increase once in next stitch, K7, repeat from * to end of round.

Rounds 52–54: Knit to end of round.

Round 55: *Increase once in next stitch, K8, repeat from * to end of round.

Rounds 56–58: Knit to end of round.

Round 59: *Increase once in next stitch, K9, repeat from * to end of round (66 sts).

Rounds 61–62: Knit to end of round.

Skirt of triangles – Side One

To work the first triangle, work moss stitch pattern on the first 11 stitches of one side and ignore the other stitches resting on the circular needles. Note that you are making one straight edge and one slanted edge on each of the triangles.

Row 1: With the RIGHT side facing and using 4 mm (UK 8, US 6) regular needles (you can use the pair of double-pointed needles if you like), *K1, P1, repeat from* 4 more times, K1 (11 sts), ***turn***.

Row 2 (working back across the last 11 stitches): *K1, P1, repeat from * to last stitch, K1.

Row 3: P2tog, *K1, P1, repeat from * to last stitch, K1.

Row 4 (and each alternate row): Continue in moss stitch pattern, knitting the purl stitches and purling the knit stitches.

Row 5: K2tog, *P1, K1, repeat from * to end of row.

Row 7: P2tog, *K1, P1, repeat from * to end of row.

Repeat Rows 4–7 until 2 stitches remain.

Cast off. Break off yarn.

Join in yarn and repeat the instructions to make 2 more triangles on the remaining stitches on the same side.

Skirt of triangles – Side Two

Join in yarn and repeat the instructions as for Side One, but this time start with the WRONG side facing. This will give a mirror image of the triangle slant on the other side.

Underbelly circle

This is a knitted circle sewn to the underside of the Cone Neck to hold the fibrefill in place.

Using both sets of 4 mm (UK 8, US 6) circular needles and Periwinkle, cast on 65 stitches (64 sts plus 1 st, for joining in the round), placing 32 stitches on one circular needle and 33 stitches on the other circular needle. Refer to **Knitting in the round on two sets of circular needles,** on page 8, to join.

Rounds 1–2: *K1, P1, repeat from * to end of round.
Round 3: *K2tog, K6, repeat from * to end of round.
Round 4 (and each alternate round): Knit to end of round.
Round 5: *K2tog, K5, repeat from * to end of round.
Round 7: *K2tog, K4, repeat from * to end of round.
Round 9: *K2tog, K3, repeat from * to end of round.
Round 11: *K2tog, K2, repeat from * to end of round.
Round 13: *K2tog, K1, repeat from * to end of round.
Round 15: K2tog to end of round.
Round 16: Knit to end of round.
Break off thread and, using a darning needle, thread end through remaining stitches and draw up tightly. Darn thread in on wrong side.

Comb – Side One

Using two 4 mm (UK 8, US 6) double-pointed needles and Red, cast on 12 stitches.
Row 1: Knit to end of row.
Row 2: Purl to end of row.
Shape first peak as follows:

Row 3: Increase once in next stitch, K2, increase once in next stitch, *turn*.

(Use the 3rd 4 mm (UK 8, US 6) double-pointed needle to work back over these last 6 sts.)

Row 4 (and each alternate row): Purl to end of row.

Row 5: K2tog, K4.

Row 7: K2tog, K3.

Row 9: K2tog, K2.

Row 11: K2tog, K1.

Row 12: Purl to end of row.

Cast off. Break off yarn.

Shape second peak as follows:

Join the yarn to the next 4 stitches with the RIGHT side (of stocking stitch) facing. Repeat Rows 3–12. Cast off and break off yarn.

Shape third peak as follows:

Join the yarn to the next 4 stitches with the RIGHT side (of stocking stitch) facing. Repeat Rows 3–12. Cast off and break off yarn.

Comb – Side Two (mirror image)

Using 4 mm (UK 8, US 6) double-pointed needles and Red, cast on 12 stitches.

Row 1: Purl to end of row.

Row 2: Knit to end of row.

Shape first peak as follows:

Row 3: Increase once in the next stitch, P2, increase once in the next stitch, *turn*.

(Use the 3rd 4 mm (UK 8, US 6) double-pointed needle to work back over these last 6 sts.)

Row 4 (and each alternate row): Knit to end of row.

Row 5: P2tog, P4.

Row 7: P2tog, P3.

Row 9: P2tog, P2.

Row 11: P2tog, P1.

Row 12: Knit to end of row.

Cast off. Break off yarn.

Shape second peak as follows:

Join the yarn to the next 4 stitches with the WRONG side (of stocking stitch) facing. Repeat Rows 3–12. Cast off and break off yarn.

Shape third peak as follows:

Join the yarn to the next 4 stitches with the WRONG side (of stocking stitch) facing. Repeat Rows 3–12. Cast off and break off yarn.

Place the two Combs together, wrong sides facing. Using a simple overcast stitch, sew the two Combs together around the edge.

Wattle

Using the 4 mm (UK 8, US 6) double-pointed needles and Red, cast on 4 stitches. Referring to the I-cord instructions on page 129, make a 20 cm (8 in) length of cord.

LOOPY BODY

Lower Body

Using both sets of 4 mm (UK 8, US 6) circular needles and Periwinkle, cast on 65 stitches (64 sts plus 1 st, for joining in the round), placing 32 stitches on one circular needle and 33 stitches on the other circular needle. Refer to **Knitting in the round on two sets of circular needles**, on page 8, to join.

Round 1: *K1, P1, repeat from * to end of round.

Round 2: *K1, P1, repeat from * to end of round.

To 'make loop'

Insert needle into next stitch, wind yarn over the needle point, then over one finger of the left hand and over the needle point again. Draw the 2 loops through the stitch and place them back on the left needle. Knit through the back of the two loops.

Round 3: *'Make loop', P1, repeat from * to end of round.

Round 4: *K1, P1, repeat from * to end of round.
Repeat rounds 3 and 4 two more times.
Round 9: *'Make loop', P1, repeat from * to end
of round.

Divide for sides as follows:
Side One
Now you will begin to work in ROWS not rounds. To
start working in rows, turn the work so that you are
working back across the stitches you have just made,
keeping the loopy ribbed pattern correct.
Row 1: *K1, P1, repeat from * to end of row.
Row 2: K1, P1, *'make loop', P1, K1, P1, repeat from
* to last 2 sts, 'make loop', P1.
Row 3: *K1, P1, repeat from * to end of row.
Row 4: *'Make loop', P1, K1, P1, repeat from * to end
of row.
Row 5: *K1, P1, repeat from * to end of row.
Repeat rows 2–5 two more times.
Row 14: K1, P1, *'make loop', P1, K1, P1, repeat from
* to last 2 st, 'make loop', P1.
Row 15: *K1, P1, repeat from * to end of row.
Leave stitches on needle. Break off yarn.

Side Two
With the right side (loop side) facing you, join yarn
to the stitches on other needle and work Side Two to
correspond with Side One.

Upper body
Referring to **Knitting in the round on two sets of
circular needles**, on page 8, begin working in ROUNDS
again as follows:

Rounds 1–6: *K1, P1, repeat from * to end of round.
Round 7: *K2tog, K1, P1, repeat from * to end of round.
Rounds 8–12: *K2, P1, repeat from * to end of round.
Round 13: *K2tog, P1, repeat from * to end of round.

Rounds 14–18: *K1, P1, repeat from * to end of round.
Break off yarn, thread end through remaining stitches,
draw up tightly and darn end in.

LINING
Lower Body
Using both sets of 4 mm (UK 8, US 6) circular needles
and MC, cast on 73 stitches (72 sts plus 1 st, for joining
in the round), placing 36 stitches on one circular needle
and 37 stitches on the other circular needle. Refer to
Knitting in the round on two sets of circular needles,
on page 8, to join.

Rounds 1–9: *K2, P2, repeat from * to end of round
(2x2 rib).

Divide for sides as follows:
Side One
Now you will begin to work in ROWS not rounds. To
start working in rows, turn the work so that you are
working back across the stitches you have just made.
Rows 1–22: Continue in 2x2 rib pattern.
Leave stitches on needle. Break off yarn, leaving a tail
to darn in later.

Side Two
Join in the yarn to the stitches on the other needle and
complete Side Two to correspond with Side One.

Upper Body
Begin working in ROUNDS again, referring to **Knitting
in the round on two sets of circular needles**, on page 8.
Round 1 (and each alternate round): Knit to end
of round.
Round 2: *K7, K2tog, repeat from * to end of round.
Round 4: *K6, K2tog, repeat from * to end of round.
Round 6: *K5, K2tog, repeat from * to end of round.

Continue in this decreasing pattern until 8 stitches remain (4 on each circular needle).
Break off yarn, thread end through remaining stitches, draw up tightly and darn in end on wrong side.

PUTTING IT ALL TOGETHER

Darn in all ends. Find the line passing through the centre of the Cone Neck, from front (teapot spout) to back (handle). The Skirt Triangles that are splayed wide apart will sit either side of the spout and the skirt triangles that are close together will sit either side of the handle.

Sew the Wattle into place on the Cone Neck, facing towards the front but perhaps at a rakish angle like mine. Sew the Comb into place directly opposite the Wattle.

Following the instructions on page 15, felt the Cone Neck (with Wattle and Comb in place.) Dry into shape by inserting a piece of light cardboard rolled into the shape of a cone. Drying might take a day or two.

Stuff the cone with fibrefill and then sew the Underbelly Circle into place.

Using black yarn, sew on the large red button eyes.

Secure the Loopy Body to the lining by sewing around the edges of the spout and handle openings.

Place the completed body on the teapot. Sit the Cone Neck on the base. Pin the fabulous feathers to the body in line with the Comb. Secure the Cone Neck and the fabulous feathers to the body.

Give your rooster a stage name worthy of his grandeur.

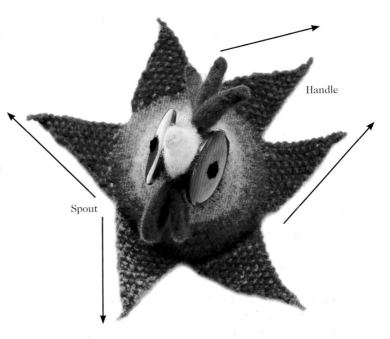

Handle

Spout

The left skirt is a mirror image of the right skirt and the comb and wattle of Pedro's head will sit off centre to the handle and spout

I could tell you that this old jumper was my father's and that my mother made it for him with love and joy and that he wore it with great pride until his dying day despite all the moth holes. I could tell you that his old jumper evokes in me oh, so nostalgic memories. I could tell you that touching it and smelling it brings tears to my eyes.

But I would be lying. I bought it at an op shop. It was a factory-made jumper. It is a lovely idea though, don't you think, giving an old loved woollen jumper a new life as a tea cosy.

The angel-fish brooch really did belong to my mother. And it does bring fond memories to mind, more often now that it is out on show.

You need to like sewing a little bit to make Sleeveless in Seattle. And the only knitting technique you need is the knit stitch.

Sleeveless in Seattle

{Recycled, sewn, knitted and dressed up}

SIZE
You can adapt this one to fit any sized teapot.

MATERIALS
- An old pure woollen jumper
- 1 x 50 g (1¾ oz) ball 8-ply from your stash
- Pretty brooch

EQUIPMENT
- One pair 5 mm (UK 6, US 8) needles
- One pair 5 mm double-pointed needles
- Darning needle
- Scissors
- Your favourite rubber gloves
- Soap

COSY

Cut the sleeves off the jumper close to the shoulder. Referring to the instructions on page 15, felt the sleeves.

When the sleeves are completely dry, cut away the frayed end (as opposed to the cuff end) of the sleeve. The size of the teapot will determine at what point in the sleeve you'll make this cut. Have the teapot in front of you to measure against.

Make a cut each for the spout and handle openings, again measuring against the teapot to get their size and position.

Sew right around the cut edges with a closely-stitched blanket stitch or a simple overcasting. It doesn't need to be super neat as the stitching will be covered with the I-cord later. It is really a matter of containing further fraying of the knitted fabric. The felting will have already helped with containing the fraying.

I-CORD

Using 5 mm (UK 6, US 8) double-pointed needles and following the instructions on page 129, make a length of I-cord to fit right around all the cut edges (that is, around both openings and around the lower edge).

LINING

The lining is a rectangle knitted on the diagonal in garter stitch using 5 mm (UK 6, US 8) needles. (Follow the instructions for the Diagonal Scarf on page 133.) There is one important thing to remember though – knit the rectangle lining long enough to fit up inside the sleeve, past the spout and handle opening cuts, to accommodate the height of the teapot.

PUTTING IT ALL TOGETHER

After sewing around the cut edges of the cosy (as above), sew the rectangle lining into place. Then, with small tacking stitches (tacking is the simplest of all the sewing stitches), secure the I-cord into place on the outside of the cosy.

Note that the cosy is only secured together (by the I-cord cross-over) under the spout, but is left to splay open under the handle.

Now it's time for dressing up: fold the sleeve down and pin with your favourite brooch.

Why use two sleeves when one will do? Because you can that's why. And look how different she is. Two sleeves with lining AND stuffing. Up in Arms is the perfect cosy for the armies of tea aficionados who go camping in the snow every winter. They do really. Don't they?

The knitting and putting together instructions are much the same as for Sleeveless in Seattle. You'll need to make some felted balls ... or use buttons or beads or tiny pompoms.

SIZE
Like Sleeveless, you can adapt this one to fit any sized teapot.

MATERIALS
- An old pure woollen jumper
- 1 x 50 g (1¾ oz) ball 8-ply wool from your stash
- Felted balls or buttons or beads
- Polyester fibrefill

EQUIPMENT
- One pair 5 mm (UK 6, US 8) needles
- One pair 5 mm (UK 6, US 8) double-pointed needles
- Darning needle
- Scissors

The essential instructions are the same as for Sleeveless in Seattle, but with a little fibrefill stuffed flat and evenly all the way up and down the sleeves. Imagine the possibilities ...

See page 128 for instructions on making felted balls.

Soxy Ladies

Ah! The inimitable hand-knitted sock! It has made a glorious comeback, warming the feet of knitters and friends of knitters the world over.

Heaven forbid that I might suggest you would tire of knitting and giving socks, but if you did find yourself looking for a little light relief, then Soxy Ladies might surprise and delight.

The following three patterns are all based on the basic construction of the sock and take advantage of the clever and beautiful self-striping sock wools available to us.

These chappies are always happiest in a crowd and as three is a crowd …

Mongolian Sock Warriors

{Knitted}

SIZE

To fit a two-cup tea pot that stands 9 cm (3½ in) tall (not including the knob) and 12 cm (4¾ in) in diameter (not including the spout and handle).

MATERIALS

- 1x 25 g (1 oz) ball 4-ply wool, Main Colour (MC): Purple
- 1x 25 g (1 oz) ball 4-ply wool, Contrast Colour 1 (CC1): Red
- 1x 25 g (1 oz) ball 4-ply variegated sock wool, Contrast Colour 2 (CC2): Brown/red/yellow
- 1 x 25 g (1 oz) ball 4-ply wool, Contrast Colour 3 (CC3): Yellow
- Firm cardboard
- Masking tape

EQUIPMENT

- Two sets 2.75 mm (UK 12, US 2) circular needles, 60 cm (24 in) long from needle tip to needle tip
- 3 mm (UK 11, US D/3) crochet hook, for finishing edges
- Darning needle
- Scissors

BODY

Lower Body

Remember! You will be working in ROUNDS and then in ROWS and things change.

Using both sets of 2.75 mm (UK 12, US 2) circular needles and MC, cast on 113 stitches (112 sts plus 1 st, for joining in the round), placing 56 stitches on one circular needle and 57 stitches on the other circular needle. Refer to **Knitting in the round on two sets of circular needles**, on page 8, to join.

Rounds 1–10: *K2, P2, repeat from * to end of round (2x2 rib).

Divide for sides as follows:

Side One

Now you will begin to work in ROWS not rounds. To start working in rows, turn the work so that you are working back across the stitches you have just made. Work Basket stitch in ROWS, thus:

Row 1: *P2, K2, repeat from * to end of row (56 sts).
Row 2: *P2, K2, repeat from * to end of row.
Row 3: *K2, P2, repeat from * to end of row.
Row 4: *K2, P2, repeat from * to end of row.
Repeat these 4 rows 6 more times (28 rows of basket stitch in total) or until the side measures to the top of the spout and handle.
Leave stitches on needle. Break off yarn, leaving a long tail to darn in later.

Side Two

Join yarn to the stitches on the other needle and work Side Two to correspond with Side One.

Crown

Begin working in rounds again, referring to **Knitting in the round on two circular needles**, on page 8.

Continue working in basket stitch for 8 rounds.
Rounds 9 and 10: Knit to end of round.
Round 11: *K2, K2tog, repeat from * to end of round.
Repeat these three rounds until 14 stitches remain.
Knit two more rounds.
Break off yarn at the end of this decreasing pattern, leaving a long tail. Using a darning needle, thread end through remaining stitches, draw up tightly and darn in end on wrong side.

TOWER

Using both sets of 2.75 mm (UK 12, US 2) circular needles and MC, cast on 65 stitches (64 sts plus 1 st, for joining in the round), placing 32 stitches on one circular needle and 33 stitches on the other circular needle. Refer to **Knitting in the round on two sets of circular needles**, on page 8, to join.

Rounds 1–14 (starting at the top cuff): *K2, P2, repeat from * to end of round (2x2 rib).
Change to CC1.
Round 15: Knit to end of round.
Rounds 16–18: Purl to end of round.
Change to the MC.
Round 19: Knit to end of round.
Rounds 20–22: Purl to end of round.
Change to CC2.
Rounds 23–34: Knit to end of round.
Change to CC1.
Round 35: Knit to end of round.
Rounds 36–38: Purl to end of round.
Change to MC.
Round 39: Knit to end of round.
Rounds 40–42: Purl to end of round.
Change to CC2.
Rounds 43–54: Knit to end of round.
Change to CC1.
Round 55: Knit to end of round.

Rounds 56–58: Purl to end of round.
Change to MC.
Round 59: Knit to end of round.
Rounds 60–62: Purl to end of round.

Divide for Side Flaps as follows:
Side Flap One
Now you will begin to work in ROWS not rounds. To start working in rows, turn the work so that you are working back across the stitches you have just made. Join in CC3 (but do not break off MC).
Row 1 (wrong side): Slip the first stitch, *P1 (CC3), P1 (MC), repeat from * to end of round.
Row 2: (right side): *Slip 1, K1 (CC3), repeat from * to end of row, weaving in MC at the back of the work as you go.
Repeat these 2 rows 15 more times (32 rows in all). Change to MC.
Row 33: *K1, P1, repeat from * to end of row.
Row 34: *P1, K1, repeat from * to end of row, forming moss stitch pattern. (This will help to stop the edge from curling up, as happens with stocking stitch.)
Row 35: *K1, P1, repeat from * to end of row.
Cast off, keeping moss stitch pattern correct.

Side Flap Two
Join in yarn to stitches on other needle and work Side Flap Two to correspond with Side Flap One.

Side Flap variation
If you want to knit the variation of the skirt on the teapot at the back of the photograph, work 32 rows as follows, after dividing for the Side Flaps, using CC2 only:
Row 1 (wrong side): Slip the first stitch, purl to end of row.
Row 2 (right side): *Slip 1, K1, repeat from * to end of row.
Repeat these 2 rows 15 more times (32 rows in all).

Change to MC.
Proceed as for Rows 33–35 of Side Flap One, above.

Side Flap Edges
Note. American crocheters, please check the Crochet Abbreviations and Conversions table on page 134.
Using MC and 3 mm (UK 11, US D/3) hook, work a row of dc along the side edges of the flaps for a neat finish. (If you don't crochet, work a red blanket stitch edging to the flap lengths instead.)

PUTTING IT ALL TOGETHER
To stiffen the tower, I have used thick cardboard, rolled up and secured to the correct cylindrical width with masking tape. It is very simple to make and is easily removed for washing.

Darn in all ends. Place the knitted body on the teapot. Position the knitted tower on the knitted body. Using running stitch, sew the tower to the body at the point where the tower meets the side flaps. This is best done with the teapot sitting on a flat surface, such as a table or a tray, to ensure that nothing goes skew-whiff.

Little Miss Cupcake is also born of the sock construction.
This is very therapeutic knitting. Four little cupcakes all joined
together with one final cupcake. Indeed, you could just make
lots of little cupcakes (see page 126).

Little Miss Cupcake

SIZE
To fit a two-cup teapot that stands 9 cm (3½ in) tall (not including the knob)
and 12 cm (4¾ in) in diameter (not including the spout and handle).

MATERIALS
- 1x 50 g (1¾ oz) ball Nundle Collection Retro 4-ply wool, Main Colour (MC):
  Kelp (green)
- 1x 50 g (1¾ oz) ball Nundle Collection Retro 4-ply wool, Contrast Colour
  1 (CC1): Peony (light pink)
- 1 x 50 g (1¾ oz) ball Nundle Collection Retro 4-ply wool, Contrast Colour
  2 (CC2): Primrose (dark pink)
- Polyester fibrefill

EQUIPMENT
- Two sets 2.75 mm (UK 12, US 2) circular needles, 60 cm (24 in) long from
  needle tip to needle tip
- Scissors
- Darning needle

SIDE CUPCAKES (MAKE 4)

Using both sets of 2.75 mm (UK 12, US 2) circular needles and MC (Kelp), cast on 9 stitches (8 sts plus 1 st, for joining in the round), placing 4 stitches on one circular needle and 5 stitches on the other circular needle. Refer to **Knitting in the round on two sets of circular needles**, on page 8, to join.

Round 1 (and each alternate round): Knit to end of round.

Round 2: Increase once in every stitch to end of round.

Round 4: *K1, increase once in next stitch, repeat from * to end of round.

Round 6: *K2, increase once in next stitch, repeat from * to end of round.

Round 8: *K3, increase once in next stitch, repeat from * to end of round.

Round 10: *K4, increase once in next stitch, repeat from * to end of round.

Round 12: *K5, increase once in next stitch, repeat from * to end of round.

Round 14: *K6, increase once in next stitch, repeat from * to end of round (64 sts).

Round 15: Knit to end of round.

Round 16: *K2, P2, repeat from * to end of round. Join in CC1 (Peony).

Round 17: *K2 (CC1), P2 (MC), repeat from * to end of round.

Rounds 18–24: As for Round 17.

Rounds 25 and 26: Using MC only, *K2, P2, repeat from * to end of round.

Join in CC2 (Primrose).

Round 27: Using two threads of CC2 only, knit to end of round. (Using two threads at this point will give the cupcake shape a very sturdy base, which is important in the tea cosy construction.)

Rounds 28–30: Purl to end of round.

Round 31: Working with one thread only, knit to end of round.

Cast off.

SIDE ONE

(For the purposes of putting it all together, think of the circle as a square with 4 sides, each side or edge being made up of 16 stitches.)

Thread a darning needle with Primrose yarn and, using mattress stitch (see below), sew 2 cupcakes together along one edge of the 'square'.

MATTRESS STITCH

Sewing with mattress stitch gives an invisible seam. Lay the two edges side by side with the right side facing you. Thread a darning needle with yarn that matches the edges you are joining. Working from bottom to top, pick up the 1st stitch (adjacent to the cast off) on the right hand cupcake and then pick up the 1st stitch (adjacent to the cast off) on the left hand cupcake. Continue working right cupcake, left cupcake, four or five times, and then pull the thread tight, drawing the edges together. The seam will magically disappear.

SIDE TWO

Sew the other 2 cupcakes together in the same manner as Side One.

TOP CUPCAKE

The top cupcake is made from the bottom up, AFTER joining the two sides together with the Peony-coloured (CC1) wool band.

It would be so easy…

… just to say to you: Using CC1 (Peony) and beginning in the top centre of Side One (where the two cupcakes join), pick up 16 stitches. Then make 8 new stitches to bridge the gap over the handle. Pick up 32 stitches on the top of Side Two. Make 8 new stitches to bridge the gap over the spout. Pick up the last 16 stitches from Side One.

But …

… then it might not look as good as it could. Now, I have said in the introduction that this little book is not a knitting techniques book. So, if the following ruminations don't make sense, please have a look elsewhere. I love my *Reader's Digest Complete Guide to Needlecraft*, from 1985. It has everything in it. And then, of course, there is the wonderful worldwide web that has everything-plus in it.

So…

… rather than picking up stitches across the top of Side One, you CAST ON stitches, pulling each new cast-on stitch from back to front of the work. The best way to cast on through the already knitted fabric is to use the 'double cast-on method' (see below). The double cast-on method employs one needle and a double length of yarn. It also works in the same direction as you knit. Right to left for right-handed knitters, and left to right for left-handed knitters.

DOUBLE CAST-ON METHOD

If you are not used to this cast-on method, you might like to try it out for a little while BEFORE using it as a 'pick up stitch' method.

Pull out about an arm's length of yarn from the ball of wool. Make a slip-knot loop at that point and place on your working needle. You only need the one needle and it will sit in the usual working position (the right hand for right-handed knitters and the left hand for left-handed knitters). The forefinger of the other hand will act as the other needle. Loop the loose length of yarn around your forefinger, insert your working needle into the loop and with the ball yarn, knit the stitch.

Back to 'It would be so easy'…

Follow the instructions under 'It would be so easy', using the double cast-on method to pick up the stitches. Insert your working needle into the first stitch of the knitted fabric edge. Cast on at the back of the work. Bring the new stitch to the front of the work. Repeat. Working the bridge across the spout and handle will be neat and strong now. Proceed as follows:

TOP PEONY-PINK BAND

Round 1 (and each alternate round): Knit to end of round.
Round 2: K18, K2tog.
Round 4: K17, K2tog.
Round 6: K16, K2tog.
Round 8: K15, K2tog.

TOP KNOT CUPCAKE

Change to CC2 (Primrose).

Round 9: Knit to end of round.

Rounds 10–12: Purl to end of round.

Change to MC (Kelp).

Round 13: Knit to end of round.

Rounds 14–15: *K2, P2, repeat from * to end of round.

Join in CC1 (Peony).

Rounds 16–23: *K2 (CC1), P2 (MC), repeat from * to end of round.

Break off CC1.

Round 24: (Using MC only) *K2, P2, repeat from * to end of round.

Round 25 (and each alternate round): Knit to end of round.

Round 26: *K6, K2tog, repeat from * to end of round.

Round 28: *K5, K2tog, repeat from * to end of round.

Round 30: *K4, K2tog, repeat from * to end of round.

Round 32: *K3, K2tog, repeat from * to end of round.

Round 34: *K2, K2tog, repeat from * to end of round.

Round 36: *K1, K2tog, repeat from * to end of round.

Round 38: K2tog to end of round.

Break off yarn and, with a darning needle, thread end though remaining stitches, draw up tightly and darn in end on wrong side.

LOWER PEONY-PINK BAND

Using CC1 (Peony), 'pick up' stitches just as you did for the Top Band.

Rounds 1–16: Knit to end of round.

Cast off LOOSELY.

CIRCULAR LIDS (MAKE 5)

The 5 circular lids are sewn to the underside of the cupcakes to keep the polyester fibrefill in place.

Cast on and work as for Rounds 1–14 of the Side Cup Cake.

Cast off.

PUTTING IT ALL TOGETHER

Darn in all ends. Fill each of the cupcakes with fibrefill. Not too much – just enough to make them sit up all perky. Then sew the circular lids in place, using MC yarn and ensuring that your stitches can't be seen on the right side of the work.

To tweak the centre of each cupcake downwards, make one stitch up through the bottom of the cupcake to the top centre and back down again and tie off.

One recently had occasion to pontificate on what one might call a group of tea cosies. One simply pontificated. It was one's clever friends that came up with a CUDDLE of COSIES. It occurs to one that it might also aptly describe a group of knitters. A CUDDLE of KNITTERS. Which begs the question, how many knitters make a cuddle? Three of course. Though a COUPLE of knitters would doubtfully stay a couple of knitters for long.

This cuddle of tea cosies looks best in self-striping sock wool.

Pot Sock Frock and Petticoat

{Knitted}

SIZE
To fit a two-cup tea pot that stands 9 cm (3½ in) tall (not including the knob) and 12 cm (4¾ in) in diameter (not including the spout and handle).

MATERIALS
- 50 g (1¾ oz) ball 4-ply self-striping sock wool (MC)
- 50 g (1¾ oz) ball 4-ply contrasting wool (CC)

EQUIPMENT
- Two sets 2.75 mm (UK 12, US 2) circular needles, 60 cm (24 in) long from needle tip to needle tip
- Scissors
- Darning needle

PETTICOAT

The Petticoat begins at the top cuff and is worked downwards in ROUNDS.

Remember! You will be working in ROUNDS and then in ROWS and things change.

Upper Body

Using both sets of 2.75 mm (UK 12, US 2) circular needles and the contrasting 4-ply wool (CC), cast on 65 stitches (64 sts plus 1 st, for joining in the round), placing 32 stitches on one circular needle and 33 stitches on the other circular needle. Refer to **Knitting in the round on two sets of circular needles**, on page 8, to join.

Rounds 1–30 (or until desired length to peek through the outer sock frock): *K2, P2, repeat from * to end of round (2x2 rib).

Round 31: *K7, increase once in next stitch, repeat from * to end of round.
Round 32 (and each alternate row): Knit to end of round.
Round 34: *K8, increase once in next stitch, repeat from * to end of round.
Round 36: *K9, increase once in next stitch, repeat from * to end of round.
Round 38: *K10, increase once in next stitch, repeat from * to end of round.
Round 40: *K11, increase once in next stitch, repeat from * to end of round.
Round 42: *K12, increase once in next stitch, repeat from * to end of round.

Divide for sides as follows:
Side One

Now you will begin to work in ROWS not rounds. To start working in rows, turn the work so that you are working back across the stitches you have just made.
Row 1: Slip the first stitch, then purl to end of row.
Row 2: *Slip 1, K1, repeat from * to end of row.
Repeat these two rows 15 more times (32 rows in total). Leave stitches on needle. Break off yarn, leaving a long tail to darn in later.

Side Two

Join in yarn to stitches on other needle and work side Two to correspond with Side One.

Lower Body

Referring to **Knitting in the round on two sets of circular needles**, on page 8, begin working in ROUNDS again as follows:
Rounds 1–12 (right side): *K1, P1, repeat from * to end of round (1x1 rib).
Rounds 13–24: Knit to end of round. (This forms a rolled stocking stitch edge along the bottom.)
Cast off.

Spout and handle rolled cuffs

Using both sets of 2.75 mm (UK 12, US 2) circular needles and with the right side facing, pick up 52 stitches evenly around the spout hole, 26 stitches on each circular needle.

Rounds 1–10: Knit to end of round.

Cast off.

Repeat for the handle hole.

OUTER GARMENT

Remember! You will be working in ROUNDS and then in ROWS and things change.

The Outer Garment begins at the top cuff and is worked downwards in ROUNDS.

Using both sets of 2.75 mm (UK 12, US 2) circular needles and the self-striping sock wool (MC), cast on 65 stitches (64 sts plus 1 st, for joining in the round), 32 on one circular needle and 33 on the other. Refer to **Knitting in the round on two sets of circular needles,** on page 8, to join.

Rounds 1–22: *K2, P2, repeat from * to end of round (2x2 rib).

Work increasing rounds as for Rounds 31–42 of Petticoat.

Work Sides One and Two as for Petticoat.

Lower Body

Referring to **Knitting in the round on two sets of circular needles,** on page 8, begin working in ROUNDS again as follows:

Rounds 1–6: Purl to end of round.

Rounds 7–12: *K1, P1, repeat from * to end of round (1x1 rib).

Cast off, keeping rib pattern correct.

PUTTING IT ALL TOGETHER

Darn in all ends. Place the Petticoat on the teapot, right side facing out. Put the Outer Garment over the Petticoat, making sure the peek-a-boo rolypoly bits of the Petticoat fold out well over the dress.

Hanky Panky should be called Easy Peasy. She is beautifully simple and simply beautiful. Well, I think so. Squares knitted in garter stitch on the diagonal. Two large squares and five small squares. That's all. Be sure to use TWO strands of wool, though. Two strands of wool make it strong and give it its 'sit up and take notice'.

Hanky Panky

{Knitted}

SIZE

To fit a two-cup teapot that stands 9 cm (3½ in) tall (not including the knob) and 12 cm (4¾ in) in diameter (not including the spout and handle).

MATERIALS

Note. You can make two cosies with five balls of wool. One ball of wool makes one large square and one small square.

- 1 x 50 g (1¾ oz) ball Nundle Collection 8-ply wool: Hot Pink
- 1 x 50 g (1¾ oz) ball Nundle Collection 8-ply wool: Light Pink
- 1 x 50 g (1¾ oz) ball Nundle Collection 8-ply wool: Amethyst
- 1 x 50 g (1¾ oz) ball Nundle Collection 8-ply wool: Purple
- 1 x 50 g (1¾ oz) ball Nundle Collection 8-ply wool: Cerise

EQUIPMENT

- One pair 5 mm (UK 6, US 8) knitting needles
- Darning needle
- Scissors

Pinch the upper edges of the large squares together into an X-shape as shown, and secure the centre of the X with a few stitches.

LARGE DIAGONAL SQUARE (MAKE 2)

Make one Amethyst square and one Purple square.

Using 5 mm (UK 6, US 8) needles and 2 strands 8-ply wool, cast on 2 stitches.
Row 1: Knit to end of row.
Row 2: Increase once in first stitch, knit to end of row.
Repeat Row 2 until there are 36 stitches.
Next row: Ssk, knit to end of row.
Repeat last row until 2 stitches remain.
Cast off.

SMALL DIAGONAL SQUARE (MAKE 5)

Make one square in each of the five colours.

Using 5 mm (UK 6, US 8) needles and 2 strands 8-ply wool, cast on 2 stitches.
Row 1: Knit to end of row.
Row 2: Increase once in first stitch, knit to end of row.
Repeat Row 2 until there are 24 stitches.
Next row: Ssk, knit to end of row.
Repeat last row until 2 stitches remain.
Cast off.

PUTTING IT ALL TOGETHER

Darn in all the loose threads. Lay the two large squares, one on top of the other. Join together at two adjoining corners with a simple single stitch. Place the squares over the teapot with the joins at the base of the spout and handle. Pinch the squares into an X-shape fitting the squares snugly around the pot and stitch into place at the centre of the X only.

Make the smaller squares into flower shapes by pinching each one in the centre of the square and stitch into place on the tea cosy.

The Ode to the Lime is an occasional tea cosy. It can be made for any occasion. Replace the lime with a gold ring for marriage, or little baby doll for new birth, or a mortarboard for graduation. My tangy lime is for Steve and the occasion of his tree bearing its first fruit – an occasion so momentous as to have a festival dedicated to it. It's true. A whole festival, a biennial event celebrated in downtown Brisbane since 2003. Limes are important too.

Ode to the Lime

{Knitted}

SIZE
To fit a two-cup teapot that stands 9 cm (3½ in) tall (not including the knob) and 12 cm (4¾ in) in diameter (not including the spout and handle).

MATERIALS
- 1 x 50 g (1¾ oz) ball Nundle Collection 8-ply wool: Orange
- 1 x 50 g (1¾ oz) ball Nundle Collection 8-ply wool: Brown
- 1 x 50 g (1¾ oz) ball Nundle Collection 8-ply wool: Lime (see *Note*, below)
- 1 x 50 g (1¾ oz) ball Nundle Collection 8-ply wool: Berry
- Polyester fibrefill
- 4 glass beads

Note. You won't need all of the Lime nor Berry, but one can never have too much wool.

EQUIPMENT
- One pair 6 mm (UK 4, US 10) knitting needles
- One pair 4 mm (UK 8, US 6) knitting needles
- Darning needle
- Scissors

LARGE DIAGONAL SQUARE (MAKE 2)

Make one Orange square and one Brown square.

Using 6 mm (UK 4, US 10) needles and 2 strands 8-ply wool, cast on 2 stitches.

Row 1: Knit to end of row.
Row 2: Increase once in first stitch, knit to end of row.
Repeat Row 2 until there are 36 stitches.
Next row: Ssk, knit to end of row.
Repeat last row until 2 stitches remain.
Cast off.

SMALL DIAGONAL SQUARE (MAKE 1)

Using 6 mm (UK 4, US 10) needles and 2 strands Lime wool, cast on 2 stitches.

Row 1: Knit to end of row.
Row 2: Increase once in first stitch, knit to end of row.
Repeat Row 2 until there are 24 stitches.
Next row: Ssk, knit to end of row.
Repeat last row until 2 stitches remain.
Cast off.

CUSHION (MAKE 1)

Referring to the instructions on page 131 and using 4 mm (UK 8, US 6) needles and Berry wool, make one Cushion.

LIME (MAKE 1)

Referring to the instructions on page 130 and using 4 mm (UK 8, US 6) needles and Lime wool, make one Lime.

PUTTING IT ALL TOGETHER

Darn in all the loose threads. Lay the two large squares, one on top of the other. Join together at two adjoining corners with a simple single stitch. Place the squares over the teapot with the joins at the base of the spout and handle. Pinch the squares into an X-shape about 5 cm (2 in) from the top (or fitting the squares snugly around the pot) and stitch into place at the centre of the X only.

Make a single stitch to join the cosy at two top corners where the colours meet.

Place the smaller square squarely on the top and lightly stitch into place. Arrange the Cushion and the Lime in position and secure everything together with a single stitch from the base of the lime down through the cushion and the cosy, tying off threads underneath.

Two squares knitted on the diagonal with 4 cubed pompoms – an evening's knit in.

Short Black with Two

SIZE
To fit a two-cup teapot that stands 9 cm (3½ in) tall (not including the knob) and 12 cm (4¾ in) in diameter (not including the spout and handle).

MATERIALS
- 2 x 50 g (1¾ oz) balls Nundle Collection 8-ply wool: Black
- Something from your stash for the cubed pompoms

EQUIPMENT
- One pair 5 mm (UK 6, US 8) knitting needles
- Darning needle
- Scissors

DIAGONAL SQUARE (MAKE 2)
Using 5 mm (UK 6, US 8) needles and 2 strands Black, cast on 2 stitches.
Row 1: Knit to end of row.
Row 2: Increase once in first stitch, knit to end of row.
Repeat Row 2 until there are 36 stitches.
Next row: K2tog, knit to end of row.
Repeat last row until 2 stitches remain.
Cast off.

CUBED POMPOMS (MAKE 4)
Referring to the instructions on page 132, make four cubed pompoms using colours from your stash.

PUTTING IT ALL TOGETHER
Darn in all the loose threads. Lay the two large squares, one on top of the other. Join together at two adjoining corners at the bottom with a simple single stitch.
At the top, fold the corners in to form a triangle shape and stitch into place. Do this on both squares. Then join the sides together just above the spout and handle. Attach the cubed pompoms.

Flowers and other fun stuff

There is so much more fun to be had than just tea cosies. Not that a tea cosy is ever 'just' a tea cosy.

Heaven forbid.

But imagine the flowers on the lapel of a cardigan. Imagine the cupcake given as a little gift of friendship, a puff of love. Imagine a bowl of knitted oranges. Imagine knitting the diagonal garter stitch lining longer and longer until you have a simply lovely scarf.

Make small. Enjoy all the little bits and pieces.

Then think big.

Rose

{Knitted}

MATERIALS

- Noro Kureyon or Noro Silk Garden
- 1 pair 4 mm (UK 8, UK 6) knitting needles

HERE'S HOW

Using 4 mm (UK 8, US 6) knitting needles and your choice of yarn, cast on 25 stitches. (You will be knitting in ROWS.)

Row 1: *K1, P1, repeat from * to end of row.

Row 2: *P1, K1, repeat from * to end of row.

Repeat these two rows once more.

Row 5: Increase once in each stitch to end of row (50 sts).

Row 6: Purl to end of row.

Row 7: Knit to end of row.

Repeat these two rows 2 more times.

Cast off.

Note. The tighter you cast off, the tighter the curl up in the flower. A medium tension is best.

Twirl with the curl so that the wrong side of the stocking stitch faces up and out. Sew it in place at the base.

really wild tea cosies

Short Leaf

{Knitted}

MATERIALS

- Nundle Collection 8-ply wool: Fern or Olive (or colours of your choice)
- 1 pair 4 mm (UK 8, UK 6) knitting needles

HERE'S HOW

Using 4 mm (UK 8, UK 6) knitting needles and 8-ply wool cast on 4 stitches.

Row 1 (and each alternate row): Purl to end of row.

Row 2: K1, increase once in each of next 2 stitches, K1.

Row 4: K2, increase once in each of next 2 stitches, K2.

Row 6: K3, increase once in each of next 2 stitches, K3.

Row 8: K4, increase once in each of next 2 stitches, K4.

Rows 9-13: Continue working in stocking stitch without increase.

Row 14: K4, ssk, K2tog, K4.

Row 16: K3, ssk, K2tog, K3.

Row 14: K2, ssk, K2tog, K2.

Row 16: K1, ssk, K2tog, K1.

Row 18: K2, ssk, K2tog.

Cast off.

Long Leaf

{Knitted}

MATERIALS
- Nundle Collection 8-ply wool: Fern or Olive (or colours of your choice)
- 1 pair 4 mm (UK 8, UK 6) knitting needles

HERE'S HOW
Using 4 mm (UK 8, UK 6) knitting needles and 8-ply wool, cast on 4 stitches.

Row 1 (and each alternate row): Purl to end of row.

Row 2: K1, increase once in each of next 2 stitches, K1.

Row 4: K2, increase once in each of next 2 stitches, K2.

Row 6: K3, increase once in each of next 2 stitches, K3.

Row 8: K4, increase once in each of next 2 stitches, K4.

Rows 9-13: Continue working in stocking stitch without increase.

Row 14: K4, ssk, K2tog, K4.

Row 16: Knit to end of row.

Row 18: K3, ssk, K2tog, K3.

Row 20: Knit to end of row.

Row 22: K2, ssk, K2tog, K2.

Row 24: Knit to end of row.

Row 26: K1, ssk, K2tog, K1.

Row 28: Knit to end of row.

Row 30: K2, ssk, K2tog.

Cast off.

Rose

{Crocheted}

MATERIALS

- Nundle Collection 8-ply wool: Cerise (or colour of your choice)
- 4 mm (UK 8, US G/6) crochet hook

Note. American crocheters, please check the Crochet Abbreviations and Conversions table on page 134.

HERE'S HOW

Using 4 mm (UK 8, US G/6) hook and 8-ply wool, make 50 chain.

Row 1 (starting at the outer edge): 1 dc into 3rd chain from hook, 1 dc into each chain to end of row.

Row 2: 2 ch (counts as first dc), 1 dc into each dc to end of row.

Row 3 (Outer petals): 2 ch, *2 tr into next dc, 2 dtr into next dc, 2 tr into next dc, sl st into dc of first row**. Repeat from * to ** 4 more times.

Row 4 (Inner petals): *2 tr into next 3 dc of previous row, sl st into dc of first row**, repeat from * to ** to end of row.

If, for some mysterious reason, you find you have a couple of stitches left over, don't fret. They will be wrapped up and hidden down inside the middle of the rose.
Roll the crocheted strip up into a spiral with the smaller petals at the centre of the rose and the larger petals on the outer.

Trumpet Flower

{Crocheted}

MATERIALS
- Noro Kureyon sock wook (or any 4-ply wool)
- 3 mm (UK 11, US D/3) crochet hook

Note. American crocheters, please check the Crochet Abbreviations and Conversions table on page 134.

HERE'S HOW

Using 3 mm (UK 11, US D/3) crochet hook and Noro Kureyon sock wool (or any 4-ply wool) make 4 chain. Join the chain into a circle with a slip stitch.

Round 1: 2 ch (counts as first dc), 5 dc into the circle gathering the end thread as you go. On finishing this round, pull the thread to close the circle.

Rounds 2 and 3: (Use a short piece of yarn in a contrasting colour to mark the beginning of the round.) 1dc into each dc.

Round 4: *2 dc into next dc, 1 dc into next dc**, repeat from * to ** to end of round.

Rounds 5 and 6: 1 dc into each dc to end of round.

Rounds 7 and 8: *2 dc into next dc, 1 dc into next dc**, repeat from * to ** to end of round.

Round 9: Slip stitch into next dc for a smooth rim. *3 ch, miss one dc, slip stitch into next dc**, repeat from * to ** to end of round.

Cut the thread and darn to the outside of the trumpet flower.

Gumnuts

{Crocheted}

MATERIALS
- 8-ply brown wool
- Small amount of yellow wool, for stamens
- 4 mm (UK 8, US G/6) crochet hook

Note. American crocheters, please check the Crochet Abbreviations and Conversions table on page 134.

HERE'S HOW

Using 4 mm (UK 8, US G/6) crochet hook and 8-ply wool make 4 chain. Join into a circle with a slip stitch.

Round 1: 2 ch (counts as first dc), 8 dc into chain circle.

Round 2: (Mark the beginning of the round with a short length of yarn in contrasting colour.) *2 dc into next dc, 1 dc into next dc, 1 dc into next dc**, repeat from * to ** to end of round.

Rounds 3–5: 1 dc into each dc to end of round.

Round 6: *Miss next dc, 1 dc into next dc, 1 dc into next dc**, repeat from * to ** to end of round.

To make the stamens, align five or six 10 cm (4 in) lengths of yellow wool and tie them tightly around the middle with another length of wool, leaving the tails long. Thread the tails into a darning needle and take the needle down through the nut and out the bottom, pulling the stamens into the nut. Secure the thread at the bottom and trim the stamens level with the top of the nut.

Cupcakes
{Knitted}

MATERIALS
- 1 x 50 g (1¾ oz) ball Nundle Collection Retro 4-ply wool: Peony
- 1 x 50 g (1¾ oz) ball Nundle Collection Retro 4-ply wool: Primrose
- 1 x 50 g (1¾ oz) ball Nundle Collection Retro 4-ply wool: Kelp
- Two sets 2.75 mm (UK12, US 2) circular needles
- Polyester fibrefill
- 1 pink bead
- Hard plastic circle (cut from an old document holder, perhaps)

HERE'S HOW
Using both sets of 2.75 mm (UK 12, US 2) circular needles and Peony, cast on 9 stitches (8 sts plus 1 st, for joining in the round), placing 4 stitches on one circular needle and 5 stitches on the other circular needle. Refer to **Knitting in the round on two sets of circular needles**, on page 8.

Round 1 (and each alternate round to Round 13): Knit to end of round.

Round 2: Increase once in each stitch to end of round.

Round 4: *K1, increase once in next stitch, repeat from * to end of round.

Round 6: *K2, increase once in next stitch, repeat from * to end of round.

Round 8: *K3, increase once in next stitch, repeat from * to end of round.

Round 10: *K4, increase once in next stitch, repeat from * to end of round.

Round 12: *K5, increase once in next stitch, repeat from * to end of round.

Round 14: *K6, increase once in next stitch, repeat from * to end of round (64 sts).

Round 15: Knit to end of round.

Break off Peony yarn, leaving length enough to darn or weave in.

Join in two threads of Primrose. (Using two threads at this point will give the cup cake shape a very sturdy rim.)

Round 16: Using two threads of Primrose, knit to end of round.

Rounds 17-19: Purl to end of round.

Break off ONE of the Primrose threads only.

Round 20: Knit to end of round.

Join in the Kelp wool.

Round 21: *K2 (Kelp), P2 (Primrose), repeat from * to end of round.

Rounds 22-34: As for Round 21.

Break off Kelp yarn.

Rounds 35-36: Using Primrose only, *K2, P2, repeat from * to end of round.

Round 37 (and each alternate round): Knit to end of round.

Round 38: *K6, K2tog, repeat from * to end of round.

Round 40: *K5, K2tog, repeat from * to end of round.

Round 42: *K4, K2tog, repeat from * to end of round.

Round 44: *K3, K2tog, repeat from * to end of round.

Round 46: *K2, K2tog, repeat from * to end of round (24 sts).

Now is the time to stuff the cupcake with fibrefill, shaping it so that top is full and the bottom tapers to a slightly smaller circumference. Insert the hard plastic circle to help with a flat bottom. Break off the yarn and draw up through the remaining 24 stitches and darn in to close off the cupcake. Sew the pink bead to the top.

Felted Balls

MATERIALS

- Wool roving (combed, unspun wool, available in a variety of colours from craft stores or on the net)
- Liquid soap

Note. To make balls of uniform size, try to start with the same amount of roving each time.

HERE'S HOW

Pull a piece of wool from a length of roving and gently pull the fibres apart to fluff up the wool.

Roll the roving into a soft ball in your hands (the finished ball will be less than half the size of the wool ball you start with). Fill a small bowl with hot water and add a few drops of liquid soap. Dip the ball in the hot, soapy water, then gently squeeze it out. Now roll the ball gently round and round in your hands – it will get smaller and harder as it starts to felt, and you can increase the pressure of your hands.

When the ball has cooled, dip it in hot water again and keep rolling. Repeat this process until the ball is small and hard, then rinse out the soap, roll again and allow to dry.

J-cord

{Knitted}

MATERIALS
- 8-ply wool
- 1 pair 4 mm (UK 8, US 6) double-pointed
  needles (or size specified in pattern)

HERE'S HOW
Using 4 mm (UK 8, US 6) double-pointed needles and
8-ply yarn, cast on 4 stitches.
*Slide the stitches to the other end of the needle. Take
the yarn across the back of the work from left to right
and knit the four stitches**. Repeat from * to ** until
you have your desired length.

Citrus Fruit

{Knitted}

MATERIALS
- 1 x 50 g (1¾ oz) ball Nundle Collection 8-ply wool: Lime, Sunshine or Tangerine (depending on the fruit)
- 1 pair 4 mm (UK 8, US 6) knitting needles

HERE'S HOW
Using 4 mm (UK 8, US 6) needles and one strand of 8-ply wool, cast on 5 stitches.

Row 1 (and each alternate row): Purl to end of row.

Row 2: Knit, increasing once in every stitch, to end of row.

Row 4: *K1, increase once in next stitch, repeat from * to end of row.

Row 6: *K2, increase once in next stitch, repeat from * to end of row.

Row 8: *K3, increase once in next stitch, repeat from * to end of row.

Row 10: *K4, increase once in next stitch, repeat from * to end of row.

Row 12: Knit to end of row.

Row 14: *K4, K2tog, repeat from * to end of row.

Row 16: *K3, K2tog, repeat from * to end of row.

Row 18: *K2, K2tog, repeat from * to end of row.

Row 20: *K1, K2tog, repeat from * to end of row.

Row 22: K2tog to end of row.

Row 23: Purl to end of row.

Cut the yarn leaving a long thread to sew up the lime.

Thread the yarn through the remaining 5 stitches and draw up tightly. With the right side facing sew up the seam of the lime keeping the stiches close and small. Leave 2 cm (¾ in) at the end of the seam open and fill the lime with fibrefill (don't be shy with the filling) before closing.

To make the ball bigger, begin by casting on 7 stitches and follow the increasing pattern as above.

To make the ball fatter, add an extra knit row in the middle.

To shape the lemon and lime, stuff the fibrefill to a point.

To shape the mandarin, stuff the fibrefill into a ball, then darn a thread from point to point to draw in.

Cushion

{Knitted}

MATERIALS

- 1 x 50 g (1¾ oz) ball Nundle Collection 8-ply wool: Berry (or colour of your choice)
- 1 pair 4 mm (UK 8, US 6) knitting needles
- Polyester fibrefill
- 4 green glass beads

HERE'S HOW
(Make 2 squares)

Using the 4 mm (UK 8, US 6) needles and one strand of Berry wool, cast on 2 stitches.

Row 1: Purl to end of row.

Row 2: Increase once in first stitch, knit to end of row.

Row 3: Increase once in first stitch, purl to end of row.

(To increase, work into the front and back of the stitch and yes, you can use this increasing method even on the alternate purl rows.)

Repeat Rows 2 and 3 until there are 28 stitches.

Next and following rows: Keeping stocking stitch pattern correct, ssk at the beginning of each row until only 2 stitches remain.

Cast off.

The stocking stitch knitted fabric will fall naturally into a diamond shape rather than a square. Give it a good stretch. Place the two squares, one on top of the other, with the fabric thread criss-crossing each other and the wrong sides facing. Pin the edges together, stretching it into a nice square shape as you go. Sew with a simple overcast stitch, leaving about 3 cm (1¼ in) along the last edge. Stuff lightly with fibrefill and sew up the gap. Make a stitch through the middle of the cushion and add a simple beaded tassel to each of the corners.

Pompoms

ROUND POMPOMS

I love my pompom maker. It is fast and easy and makes fabulous pompoms, but if you want to do it the old way, here's how:

Cut 2 flat donut shapes from cardboard. Align the 2 donuts and make a slit across both. (This makes it easier to remove the cardboard discs and means that you can use them again.)

Wind wool evenly around the donuts until the centre hole is almost filled, then use a tapestry needle to take the thread end through the diminishing hole.

Slide the blade of your scissors between the two circles at the outer edge and cut the yarn all the way round.

Wrap a strand of matching yarn tightly around the centre, between the two cardboard discs, and tie it off securely.

Slide the cardboard circles off the pompom and fluff it up into a ball. Trim any unruly ends, but leave the yarn ties extending for attaching the pompom.

CUBED POMPOMS

Well, of course, cubed pompoms are round pompoms snipped into shape. Imagine all the possible shapes. Do you remember making soap sculptures as a kid? We could start a whole new craze – pompom sculptures.

Scarf

{Knitted on the diagonal}

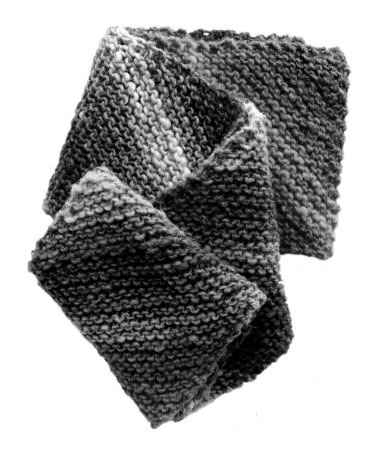

MATERIALS
- Nundle Collection 8-ply wool (amount will depend on desired length of scarf)
- 1 pair 4 mm (UK 8, US 6) knitting needles

HERE'S HOW
Using 4 mm(UK 8, US 6) needles and 8-ply wool, cast on 2 stitches.

Following Diagram below:

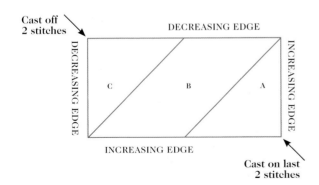

A: Increase once in first stitch of every row until you have the desired width of scarf.

B: Pattern in multiples of two rows, thus:

Row 1: Increase once in first stitch, knit to end of row.

Row 2: Ssk, knit to end of row.

Repeat these two rows until desired length of scarf.

C: Ssk at the beginning of every row until 2 stitches remain.

Cast off.

Abbreviations

Knitting Abbreviations

Abbrev	Explanation
K	knit
P	purl
st/s	stitch/es
tog	together
mm	millimetre/s
in	inch/es
RS	right side
WS	wrong side
MC	main colour
CC	contrasting colour
garter st	garter stitch (knit every row)
st st	stocking stitch (1 row knit, 1 row purl)
ssk	slip slip knit (Slip 1 stitch knitwise, slip a second stitch knitwise, then insert the left needle through the front of both slipped stitches from left to right and knit them together. This method of decreasing makes the stitches slant to the left.)
K2tog	knit two together. This method of decreasing makes the stitches slant to the right.
Increase once in next stitch	knit (or purl, if you are on a purl row) into the front and back of the next stitch.

Crochet Abbreviations and Conversions

Abbrev	Australia / NZ / UK	Abbrev	US
ch	chain	ch	chain
sl st	slip stitch	slip st	slip stitch
dc	double crochet	sc	single crochet
htr	half treble	hdc	half double crochet
tr	treble	dc	double crochet
dtr	double treble	tr / trc	treble / triple crochet
triptr	triple treble	dtr / dtrc	double treble / double triple crochet
quadtr	quadruple treble	trip tr / tr trc	triple treble / triple triple crochet

Yarns – Guidelines Only

AUSTRALIA / UK	US	TENSION / GAUGE
3-ply, 4-ply, 5-ply, jumper weight	fingering	32-26 sts to 10 cm (4 inches)
8-ply, dk, double knit	sport weight - double knit	22-24 sts to 10 cm (4 inches)

Stockists

Nundle Woollen Mill
1 Oakenville Street
Nundle NSW Australia 2340
1300 666 712 or + 61 2 6769 3330
www.nundle.com.au

Wool Addiction
6 Bundaroo Street
Bowral NSW Australia 2576
+61 2 4862 4799
www.wooladdiction.com.au

Acknowledgments

The Tea Cosy Fans

Tea cosies are important. But it turns out the people who make them and give them are much more important. I know this because the stories you tell me are not really tea cosy stories at all. They are stories about much-loved grandmothers and aunts and best friends. They are stories of fond memories. They are stories of love. Soppy, but true.

And all hail the tea cosy lovers! Thank you for playing with me with such good cheer.

The Bookish People

All hail Murdoch Books. And Diana Hill who sealed my contract with a bottle of French champagne! And Jared Fowler who photographed every tea cosy as if it were his own baby child. And Sam Moiler who styled every photo with the flair of a master. And Hugh Ford whose design wowed me. Yes Hugh. Wowed me. And Katrina O'Brien who directed us all in her quietly persuasive way.

The Editor

And all hail Georgina Bitcon, my hugely talented and long-suffering editor, who forced me to be the best I could be.

The Bloke

All hail The Bloke (aka Julian Pepperell) who loves everything I make which makes me think he is no judge at all, but pleases me extremely well. Luv ya Darls. You are solid gold.

The Friends

All hail my friends who make me laugh and cry and live. Alex, Andrea, Anne, Carolyn, Dawn, Ellen, Gayle, Glenda, Hari, Heather, Jeni, John, Julie, Lindy, Mark, Merryn, Mitchell, Nicole, Rose, Steve, Sue, Vicky and Wendy, who seem to like to organise themselves alphabetically.

The Knitting in the Round on Two Circular Needles Guru

All hail Cat Bordhi for sharing her knitting in the round on two circular needles technique with the world in her book *Socks Soar on Two Circular Needles*.

And Finally a Blog Roll

The Queen of the Tea Cosies (that's me) www.grandpurlbaa.com … … would like to thank these funny people who may not realise it, but they too have held my hand, if only for a glorious moment, in the walk towards this new book.

The Tea Cosy Aficionados (that's you)
www.wildforteacosies.blogspot.com

Henrietta (a funny chook) www.lifeinthedome.blogspot.com

The King of the Lime Festival (a born again tea cosy)
www.mymissinglife.blogspot.com

Ms Textual (an un-retiring retiree)
www.bookmarked.typepad.com/ms_textual

grrl + dog (a knit graffiti artist) www.dneese.blogspot.com

Published in 2010 by Murdoch Books Pty Limited

Murdoch Books Australia
Pier 8/9
23 Hickson Road
Millers Point NSW 2000
Phone: +61 (0) 2 8220 2000
Fax: +61 (0) 2 8220 2558
www.murdochbooks.com.au

Murdoch Books UK Limited
Erico House, 6th Floor
93–99 Upper Richmond Road
Putney, London SW15 2TG
Phone: +44 (0) 20 8785 5995
Fax: +44 (0) 20 8785 5985
www.murdochbooks.co.uk

Publisher: Diana Hill
Photographer: Jared Fowler
Stylist: Sam Moiler
Designer: Hugh Ford
Project Editor: Katrina O'Brien
Editor: Georgina Bitcon

National Library of Australia Cataloguing-in-Publication Data
Author: Prior, Loani
Title: Really wild tea cosies / Loani Prior
ISBN: 9781741966312 (pbk.)
Subjects: Tea cosies. Knitting--Patterns. Crocheting--Patterns.
Dewey Number: 746.43041

A catalogue record for this book is available from the British Library.

PRINTED IN CHINA
Reprinted 2010

STOCKISTS

Nundle Woollen Mill
1 Oakenville Street
Nundle NSW 2340
1300 666 712 or + 61 2 6769 3330
www.nundle.com.au

Wool Addiction
6 Bundaroo Street
Bowral NSW 2576
+61 2 4862 4799
www.wooladdiction.com.au